MW00799598

Hot Springs
of
North Carolina

Della Hazel Moore

ISBN 1-57072-240-4
First Edition Copyright © 1992 by Della Hazel Moore
Second Edition Copyright © 2002 by Della Hazel Moore
Printed in the United States of America
All Rights Reserved

1 2 3 4 5 6 7 8 9 0

CONTENTS

This book is dedicated with love to my friend,
Elizabeth Rumbough Baker Dotterer.

Acknowledgements

My warmest gratitude goes to Elizabeth Rumbough Baker Dotterer of whom I am particularly indebted. I am deeply grateful to the following whose guidance and suggestions were invaluable: Barney Offerman, Jan Offerman, and Lois Church Moore. Many thanks are due to Betsy Ross Neilson, Neilson historian, for her cooperation and sharing of the history of the first family of Hot Springs. I am grateful to my typist, Martha Fleming Kirkpatrick, also my friend and schoolmate, Bernice Luntsford Wright. I am deeply indebted to Karen Stieke of Wembley, Alberta, Canada, for obtaining information concerning Robert and Natika Garrett, also to Doreen Sieker of Wembley.

I would like to thank the following: David Cuningham, Rev. Andrew V. Graves, S. J., Dr. Evelyn Underwood, Mary Lee Smith, Ruth Smith, Nancy Lippard, Michelle Wyatt, Myra Hildebrandt, Steve Burns and Tayna Henderson of the U. S. Forest Service, Betty Smith, Louise Anderson, Richard H. Doughty, Mr. and Mrs. H. W. Close, Naomi Thompson, Rev. Vince Alegia, S. J., Rev. David Hinchen, S. J., James and Dot Gentry, Ed Gentry, John Lewis and Peggy Moore, Bonnie Kirby, Ethel Sprinkle, Harriet Runnion, Alma Fowler, Vera Sumerel, Sister Roberta, Sidney Harrison, Kelly Graham, Dorothy Risher, Terry Holt, Fred Tolley, Bill Culbertson, Bill and Lillian Whitten, Alberta Benninger, Bobby and Helen Ponder, Seth Metcalf, Frances Strom, Mamie Parks, Katherine Ferguson, Debra Lark and Jena Lee Buckner of the Madison County Deed Office, Ladies of the Buncombe County Deed Office, Pack Memorial Librarians, and Madison County Librarians. Lois Chandler, Mary Brooks, and Margie Bedenbaugh. Bill Barutio, Mary Pruett, Kristine Joseph, Mary Gahagan, Clyde Parks.

Preface

This is a story about the small town of Hot Springs, North Carolina —and persons who helped create it, people living in it during its periods of growth and prosperity, as well as decline and depression, and current residents of the town who have confidence and hope in its future. Especially important in recording an anecdotal history of Hot Springs are the unique family stories, the local and regional events that served as milestones in its history, the tales (both authentic and apocryphal) of individual heroics and individual misdeeds, and above all, a singular recounting of how a town and its people survive and even prevail — through floods and fires, job prosperity and job loss, high hopes and near despair.

Since I have been a resident of Hot Springs from about the age of one, and because of an abiding interest in its historical heritage, I have wanted for a long time to write an informal record of its progress, covering its two-hundred-year history.

My grandparents lived near Hot Springs in 1881, through the years of their married life. They operated a water ground grist mill for nearly forty years. My parents lived in the town or nearby for sixty-three years. Burnett Moore, my father, went to work for Colonel and Mrs. James Rumbough at the age of fourteen. A close and valued relationship developed between my father and the Rumboughs, the founding family of Hot Springs. Mrs. Rumbough called my dad "her Burnie" and it was an informal and mutually good employer-employee relationship.

I remember the five Rumbough daughters. Their stories in particular add to the fascination of Hot Springs and Madison County history. One of the daughters, Mrs. Bessie Johnson Safford, who returned to Hot Springs in the 1890's, provided much of the interesting history of that second generation of the Rumbough family.

Her niece, Elizabeth Rumbough Baker Dotterer (known affectionately as "Miss Peggy" to Hot Springs people), has been a dear friend practically all of my life. She has provided much of the link with the past, having an excellent memory for detail, as well as descriptive images of persons, places, and things, that have enriched our history.

This informal biography of a town is not intended to be the last word on its history or a highly researched and documented narrative. Rather, it's an affectionate recounting through personal testimony, public and private peers, of the pilgrimage of a town and its people — a journey involving triumph, tragedy, and sorrow.

RACING WATERS
Warm Springs, N. C.

"Racing Water," who can paint thee,
With thy scenery wild and grand?
It would take a magic pencil
Guided by a master hand.

Here are towering rugged mountains,
Granite rocks all scarred and gray,
Nature's altars whence here incense
Floats in wreaths of mist away.

At their feet thy murmuring waters
Now are singing songs of praise.
Or in sounding notes triumphant
A majestic pean raise.

Down the canon's rocky gorges
Now they wildly madly sweep,
As with laughing shout exultant
O'er the rocks they joyous leap.

Then in calm and limpid beauty
Still and deep they silent flow,
With the verdant banks o'erhanging
Pictured in the depths below.

Pulsing from the heart of Nature,
Here thy "Warm Springs" genial gush,
There, like stream from Alpine glacier,
Down the mountain coldly rush.

Tah-lee-os-tee — Racing Water —
Was thy sonorous Indian name.
But as "French Broad" thou are written
On the white man's roll of fame.

Perish that! But live the other!
For on every dancing wave
Evermore is shown the beauty
Of the name the red man gave.

— MARY BAYARD CLARKE

Mary Boulton Barden of New Bern, North Carolina, great-granddaughter of Mary Bayard Clarke, relates that her great-grandmother was a writer and editor in the l9th century. She spent several months as a guest of Dr. William Howerton at the Patton Hotel, probably in 1882. It was during this visit that she wrote the poem "Racing Waters."

She was born in 1827 and died in 1886. Mrs. Clarke's son, Willie, married Dr. William Howerton's daughter, Bessie.

There are four versions of how the French Broad River got its name. The river was supposed to have been surveyed by a man named French. It was called French Broad to distinguish it from another Broad River near Chimney Rock.

Charles Lanman visited the Patton's Warm Springs Hotel in June, 1848. He writes that the original Indian name of the French Broad was Pse-li-co. He was not able to ascertain the meaning. Its English name was derived from a famous hunter named French.

The Indian name Tahkiostie is not in the Cherokee language today, except the "ostie," which means good. Another name, Tah-kee-os-tee, is believed to mean Racing Waters.

French Broad River
(Photo Sydney Izlar)

Hot Springs, North Carolina
View from Lover's Leap
(Photo Steve Cameron)

Geography

Nestled in a lovely valley surrounded by the Pisgah National Forest, in the Southern Appalachian Mountains where the Blue Ridge joins the Great Smokies, is the town of Hot Springs. It is protected by sheltering peaks which rise abruptly on all sides. The beautiful French Broad River flows through a portion of the town and runs northwest into Tennessee. Spring Creek, a mountain stream, flows through the town. The altitude is 1360 feet and the population numbers about 750. The climate is ideal for this section of Western North Carolina, and being located in the pine wood region, there is less factory pollution, therefore, the air is purer.

In the spring and summer the mountainsides are covered with every shade of green. The sarvis (service) trees are the first to bloom, followed by the redbud, dogwood, wild azalea, rhododendron, and mountain laurel. The mountains and Appalachian Trail are brightened by a myriad of wild flowers. The trailing arbutus, Jack-in-the-pulpit, trillium, dwarf iris, lady slipper, and one of the rarest wild flowers in America, the Oconee Bells (Shortia galacifolia), was discovered by Michaux, a French botanist. It is a low, attractive perennial having glossy evergreen leaves resembling those of galax, which is also a member of the same family. It grows along the stream banks in rich woods. These are just a few of the 2945 species of flowering plants of North Carolina. Some of the plants start blooming in February. Different varieties of flowers bloom all through the spring until July.

In the fall, the multitude of colors are beyond description, ranging in shades of bright yellow, red, orange, and russet. The colors all blend in with the pine trees and dark green leaves of the mountain laurel and rhododendron, which stay green all winter.

The Appalachian Trail runs through Hot Springs. According to Dennis Schaffer, Administrator of the Trust for Appalachian Lands, "it is one of the finest Appalachian Trail towns from Georgia to Maine. This portion of the trail for most of its length, 193 miles, follows the North Carolina and Tennessee border. Much of the route is ridge crest travel with considerable distance near five thousand feet elevation. This is one of the highest and most rugged segments of the entire Appalachian chain. It features many panoramic views."

Hot Springs has a hunting season for deer, bear, and wild turkey. Small game, such as squirrel, rabbit, quail, grouse, raccoon, opossum, groundhog, and fishing, are hunted in their season.

"When them hills is hazey,
And getting teched with colors as they do,
there is something tantalizing bout
them mountains, that's surprising, and
I reckon it mought unsottle you.

Some say us folks is lazy,
but when them hills is hazey,
you can't help shirking that
dog-gone steady working to go
fooling around the mountain with a gun." [1]

---

[1] Poem written by guest at Mountain Park Hotel,
contributed by Elizabeth Rumbough Baker Dotterer.

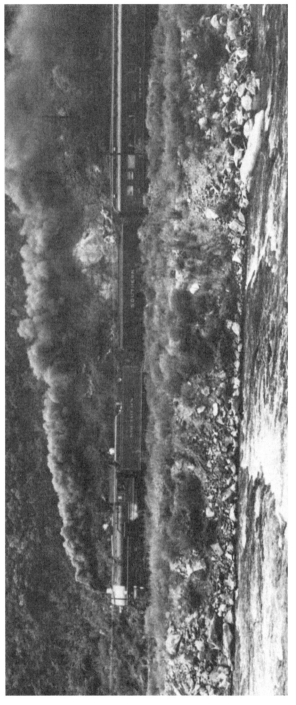

Southern Railway's Number 4501 steam engine train underway along the French Broad River. (Photo Edward L. Dupuy) *The State.*

History 1778

The warm springs on the French Broad River were discovered in 1778, according to J. G. Ramsey, historian, in his ANNALS OF TENNESSEE. Captain Logan, with a band of mountaineer riflemen and a handful of parched corn, were sent from the besieged Kentucky Fort at Boonesboro to seek supplies and reinforcements at Holston, Tennessee. Logan's two scouts, Henry Reynolds and Thomas Morgan, were kept out in advance of the settlement to watch the movements of the Indians. They had pursued some stolen horses to the river. Leaving their horses on the north bank, they waded across the river. On the southern shore, they were surprised to find the water warm. They spread news of their discovery.

It is not known how many years the warm springs had been used. The Cherokee Indians had used the springs, as they left evidence such as pieces of copper and Indian arrowheads, especially near the river. They believed in the curative powers of the warm water and they were also the masters of the western part of the state. About six years after the discovery, Gaser Dagy bought a land grant which included the springs.

The Chunn's Tavern was located on the French Broad River near the Drover's Road. The Inn was in use some 150 years before it was razed about 1931. It was infamous as the site of many robberies and murders.
(Courtesy of Pack Memorial Public Library)

15

"LOVER'S LEAP." IN THE HEART OF THE BLUE RIDGE MOUNTAINS

A SCENE AT HOT SPRINGS, N. C.

(Photo Asheville Post Card Co., Asheville, N.C.)

Legends

Not far from the springs stands a very high rock overlooking the French Broad River. It can be ascended by a narrow path through the bushes. From its summit there is a beautiful panoramic view. The river can be seen winding its way for several miles. There are two legends about this rock, which has been named Lover's Leap.

An Indian brave and maiden, Wana and Luna, were supposed to have fallen in love, but being of different tribes, they were not permitted to marry. So they decided to join hands and leaped into the river.

Another version that may have been forgotten is a booklet, HOT SPRINGS PAST AND PRESENT, by Sally Royce Weir, published in 1906. She wrote about Lone Wolf, a mighty chief of the Cherokee, who ruled the warm springs beside the Tahkiostie (French Broad River). He had three sons and one daughter, a beautiful maiden whose name was Mist-on-the-Mountain. Many braves loved her, but she was not interested in any of them. Her father wanted her to marry Tall Pine, a powerful brave, much older than she. He had threatened to become a rival in power to Lone Wolf. While they were visiting the springs, another old chief and some braves, who lived many miles away, came as friends to visit Lone Wolf, bringing beautiful gifts.

Magwa, one of the strangers, a tall, handsome young brave, fell in love with Mist-on-the-Mountain. She returned his love. Magwa on the eve of his departure asked her father for her hand, but was refused and was told that she was already promised.

On that bright June night, Mist-on-the-Mountain left camp and made her way to the foot of the towering rock. She waited and listened for Magwa, but there was no sound, except what was common to the night. She did not know that something very dangerous was hidden in the bushes watching her. She heard the dip of a paddle and a canoe touched the bank. As the figure stooped to tie the canoe, the rival brave, who had followed Mist-on-the-Mountain, unseen by the lovers, had reached the bank. As Magwa arose, Tall Pine struck him across the head, crushing his skull. He fell back lifeless into the canoe. Mist-on-the-Mountain was terrified. When the murderer approached her, she ran up the steep path to the top of the rock. He pursued her, but she was light on her feet and could run very fast. She could hear the water dashing against the base of the rock. She saw the canoe floating down the river with her lover. His spirit called back to her to keep her promise. She stood far out on the extreme point of the rock and suddenly leaped into the river. They started on their journey together. What about Tall Pine? He stood like one stunned, cold fear at his heart with that vision of sudden death. He turned in mad haste to leave the dreadful scene. He was once a great hunter, but that was all forgotten. He did not see a tawny form crouched close on an overhanging limb above him, nor those eyes of fire watching him. The moment he is under the tree limb there is a spring. A piercing cry, a heavy body of a panther struck him on the shoulders.

Sharp teeth and claws sank deep into his flesh. With a dreadful cry, beast and man rolled down the dark path. Everything was quiet except the lap of the water against the rock, and the crunching of bones in the dark rhododendron.

Do the spirits of those lovers haunt the rock? Three friendly moonshiners, Sam Hootenpile, Jim Carver, and Buck Forehand, certainly believe in spirits.

One night during the full moon, July 7, 1875, they were bringing jugs of mountain dew to exchange for corn meal to be taken to their hidden still in the mountains. They were drinking more than they were accustomed to. They claimed they saw the lover's scene acted out before their eyes. They left their jugs behind as they ran from the rock.

With the coming of the white men, the Indian trail by the river became a stage route and stock road. It became known as the Drovers Road. The first wagon from Asheville, North Carolina, to Tennessee via Warm Springs (Hot Springs) was in 1794.

The Buncombe Turnpike, built in 1828, linked North Carolina to Tennessee. The legislature directed James Patton, Samuel Chunn, and George Swain to receive a written consent for the purpose of laying out and making a turnpike road from Saluda Gap, in the county of Buncombe, by way of Smith's, Murrayville, Asheville, and Warm Springs to the Tennessee line. William P. Blair of Asheville operated the early stagecoach line, The French Broad, from Asheville to Tennessee.

The traffic over this road was heavy. The Drovers would drive cattle, horses, hogs, and other animals over this route. Large wagons with eight or ten horses would transport merchandise over the road. Some of the travelers would trade animals for a night's lodging at stage stops along the way. There were traps made on the road to steal some of the animals. One unique way was a trap with a pivot door. When an animal stepped on it, it would fall below into a box or pen. This road was very dangerous, as many people were robbed and some were murdered. The French Broad River was on one side and dense bushes were on the other. It was easy for a robber to conceal himself.

Another legend by Sally Royce Weir, HOT SPRINGS, PAST AND PRESENT, is about a traveler who had a thrilling experience. This stockman had been south with a large herd of stock and had sold them for a good profit, which he had concealed in his clothes. In those days people wore money belts. He was trying to reach a safe stage stop before dark, when his horse cast a shoe. He had to stop at the first house he came to, which did not look very inviting. After his horse was taken to the barn, he went inside the log house. He saw several weird looking men and a woman who was cooking. After eating his supper of chicken and corn bread, one of the men lit a candle and led the way up a rickety stairway to a room above. The man set the candle down on a table and said goodnight. He went out the door, closed it, turned the key softly, locking the man inside. The room was small, one bed, an old-fashioned one with a flounce around the bottom, two chairs, and a table. He looked around the room and saw a very small window that was nailed down.

There was no way to escape through it. He got the feeling that he was not alone. After taking his coat off and preparing for bed, he noticed something on the floor. He touched his finger to it and discovered that it was blood. He walked over to the table to get the candle, and with shaking hands he raised the flounce. Merciful heavens! There was a dead man still warm and bleeding. His throat had been cut from ear to ear. He very quietly turned the bedcovers down, lifted the poor man up, and put him in the bed. He turned his face toward the wall and covered him. He blew out the candle and pulled off his shoes, then stationed himself against the wall near the door, so when the door opened he would be behind it. He waited for some time, which seemed like years, when he heard the men coming up the stairs. Someone turned the key in the lock and the door was gently opened. The traveler crept through the open door. Hearing the blows that were intended to end his life, he hurried down the stairs and went outside, where he hid in the bushes. He finally reached a respectable house and returned with help, but the murderers had fled after they realized that he had escaped.

This is a true experience of another traveler who was on the road and was overtaken by darkness. He stopped at a farmer's house and asked for a night's lodging. The farmer made the traveler welcome and gave him a good supper. Afterwards, they sat in front of a warm fire and talked. The traveler asked the farmer if he would read some verses from the Bible before going to bed. The farmer got his Bible and started quoting scripture. The traveler noticed the Bible was upside down. He said, "Sir, your Bible is upside down." The farmer replied, "That is all right, I read left-handed."

The use of this road for driving stock south was continued for many years. With the coming of the railroad, Hot Springs had a stockyard that was called West Yard, a shipping point of the railroad for cattle, sheep, and hogs.

History 1783
Land Grants, William Neilson, Sr.

Gaser Dagy bought a land grant number 668, October 30, 1783, for the sum of ten pounds per hundred acres. This tract of land containing two hundred acres is located on the south side of the French Broad River. It included the warm springs and what is now the town of Hot Springs. At this time this land was in Greene County. This grant was signed at Fairfield by Esquire Samuel Johnston, captain and commander-in-chief of Fairfield. (Buncombe County Deed Book 4, p. 107.) Greene County is now in Tennessee.

Gaser Dagy sold this same two-hundred-acre tract of land on the south side of the French Broad River to John Singleton for two hundred pounds on October 3, 1784. One month and thirteen days later, on December 15, 1784 , Singleton sold this tract of land to George Hopkins. Three months and three days later, on March 28, 1785, Hopkins sold this tract of land to Isaac Taylor. (Buncombe County Deed Book A, pp. 495-496.) Twenty-three years later, on February 15, 1808, the heirs of Isaac Taylor sold this tract of land to William Neilson, Sr., for two hundred pounds. (Buncombe County Deed Book A, pp. 493-494.)

Later, on February 23, 1814, William Neilson, Sr., sold the two-hundred-acre tract which he had bought from the heirs of Isaac Taylor to his son, William Neilson, Jr., for $8000. He also deeded him a part of his estate containing 428 acres "with love and affection." He reserved a tract of land on the north side of the river, opposite and below the warm springs, for his family and heirs as long as they lived (Garrett Farm). (Buncombe County Deed Book G, pp. 141-142.)

Phillip Hale Neilson, on April 27, 1829, sold to Green K. Cessna his undivided half of the warm springs tract which was bequeathed to him from his father, William Neilson, Jr., for $8000, except the reservation contained in the deed from his grandfather, William Neilson, Sr. These tracts of land were located on both sides of the French Broad River. (Buncombe County Deed Book 16, pp. 74-75.)

At this same time, on April 27, 1829, Green K. Cessna sold to Phillip Hale Neilson all the land he owned — six tracts in the neighborhood of the Painted Rock, three miles below the warm springs, which he (Cessna) inherited from his father (663 acres for $4000). This included three islands in the French Broad River. One island was called Gables Island. (Buncombe County Deed Book 16, p. 74.)

Joseph L. Chunn and wife, Catherine, of the county of Jackson, state of Tennessee, appear on the scene. On December 6, 1831, Green K. Cessna and and the Chunns sold to James W. Patton and John E. Patton four hundred twenty-eight acres of land on the south side of the French Broad River, including the warm springs, for the sum of $20,666. (Buncombe County Deed Book 16, pp. 413-414).

John E. Patton, James A. Patton, N. W. Woodfin, and Thomas Patton, Executors of James A. Patton of Buncombe County, deeded to Joseph A. McDowell of Madison County on September 1, 1862, the two-hundred-acre tract of land on the south side of the French Broad River, which included the Patton Hotel and all the land where Hot Springs is located today, for the sum of $25,000. (Madison County Deed Book D, pp. 129-130.)

Joseph A. McDowell of Buncombe County, on October 20, 1866, sold to Carrie T. Rumbough of Warm Springs, for the sum of $45,000, four tracts of land on the south side of the French Broad River, including the entire town of Warm Springs, and one tract of one hundred fifty acres lay along Spring Creek. (Madison County Deed Book D, pp. 124-125).

It was safer to make the deed in Carrie Rumbough's name because the property of many Confederate men had been confiscated.

The Stokley-Donaldson grant number 1347 took place in 1795. This grant consisted of 60,400 acres, beginning in Cocke County and extending over the mountains to Bonnie Hill, Bluff Mountain, Pine Creek, Doe Branch, Spring Creek, and Meadow Fork.

"This grant was laid on land now lying in Cocke County as well as Madison, then described as being Greene County. Nearly one-half lay in North Carolina." [2]

John Gray Blount owned many acres of land in Madison County. He purchased two grants. Grant number 253 contained 320,640 acres. Grant number 591 contained 10,240 acres of land. He purchased these grants on March 3, 1799. He owned land near Hot Springs. He sold two hundred twenty-eight acres on December 10, 1803, to William Neilson, Sr. Blount's grants extended to Walnut, Rich Mountain, Laurel, Belva, White Rock, and Shelton Laurel to the Tennessee line.

---

[2] "Some Unwritten History," by A.B.W., 1899 Newspaper.

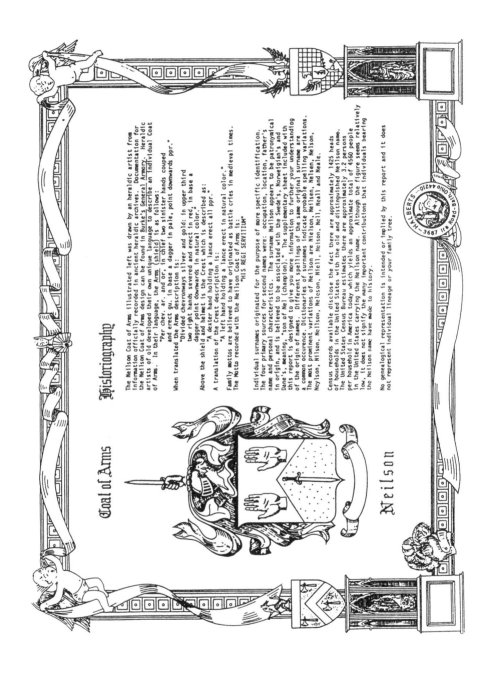

Coat of Arms

Historiography

The Neilson Coat of Arms illustrated left was drawn by an heraldic artist from information officially recorded in ancient heraldic archives. Documentation for the Neilson Coat of Arms design can be found in Burke's General Armory. Heraldic artists of old developed their own unique language to describe an individual Coat of Arms. In their language, the Arms (shield) is as follows:

"Per chev. ar. and or, in chief two sinister hands couped and erect gu. in base a dagger in pale, point downwards ppr."

When translated the Arms description is:

"Divided chevronways silver and gold; in upper third two right hands severed and erect in red, in base a dagger point downwards in natural color."

Above the shield and helmet is the Crest which is described as:

"A dexter hand holding a lance erect all ppr."

A translation of the Crest description is:

"A left hand holding a lance erect in natural color."

Family mottos are believed to have originated as battle cries in medieval times. The Motto recorded with the Neilson Coat of Arms is:

"HIS REGI SERVITIUM"

Individual surnames originated for the purpose of more specific identification. The four primary sources for second names were: occupation, location, father's name and personal characteristics. The surname Neilson appears to be patronymical in origin, and is believed to be associated with the Swede's, Norwegian's and Dane's, meaning, "son of Nel (champion)." The supplementary sheet included with this report is designed to give you more information to further your understanding of the origin of names. Different spellings of the same original surname are a common occurence. Dictionaries of surnames indicate probable spelling variations. The most prominent variations of Neilson are Nielson, Neilsen, Nelsen, Nelson, Neylson, Nilson, Noilson, Neilson, Niell, Noison, Neil, Noall and Neale.

Census records available disclose the fact there are approximately 1425 heads of households in the United States with the old and distinguished Neilson name. The United States Census Bureau estimates there are approximately 3.2 persons per household in America today which yields an approximate total of 4560 people in the United States carrying the Neilson name. Although the figure seems relatively low, it does not signify the many important contributions that individuals bearing the Neilson name have made to history.

No genealogical representation is intended or implied by this report and it does not represent individual lineage or your family tree.

Neilson

William Neilson, Sr.

William Neilson, Sr., is the founding father of Warm Springs. He was born in Ayshire, Scotland, on January 5, 1748. He was the grandson of Hugh and Katherine Douglas of Garrotan, Scotland. He married Jane Lewis in 1771. She was from Leesburg, Louden County, Virginia. He was twenty-three years old and she was nineteen. Jane was a relative of George Washington on the maternal side. Neilson's family records are on file in a Presbyterian Church in Scotland. Since he was a good friend of Bishop Asbury, he became a Methodist. He was a Lieutenant General during the Revolutionary War. He and his wife lived in Leesburg for several years before coming to Warm Springs. His two brothers, Hugh and Archibald Douglas, came to America with him.

William and Jane had fifteen children. Elizabeth, born in 1772, died as an infant. The second child was named Elizabeth after the first child. She was born in 1773. She married John Cessna of Natches, Mississippi. The Cessna's home is an historical landmark in Natches. They had family roots in Warm Springs. Robert was born in 1775. Patrick, born in 1777, died as a child. William, Jr., was born March 15, 1779. He married Sally or Holly Hale. She was his second cousin and died in childbirth in 1815. William, Jr., died in 1816. It is believed that he was buried in Johnson City, Tennessee. Their son was Phillip Hale, who sold the Warm Springs property to Green K. Cessna. Ann Neilson, born in 1781, married Colonel George Gillespie, a well-known gunsmith from Tennessee. Charles Binns was born in 1786. Sally Lewis, born in 1789, married Judge Joshua Forman of Syracuse, New York. He was killed by a Union soldier, December 17, 1863, presumedly near the gate at the Tom Garrett Inn. Thomas Lewis was born in 1791. Archibald Douglas, born in 1793, married Eliza Lynes of Charleston, South Carolina. They settled at Oven Creek, Tennessee, where they owned 1300 acres of land on the Nolichucky River. Before Captain Kirk became a renegade, he helped Archibald build a barn. During the Civil War, he came back and burned it. Archibald's son came back to North Carolina. He is buried at Weaverville, North Carolina. Nancy was born in 1795. Mary Louise was born in 1797. Jane Harriet was born in 1800. She married James R. Garrett of Edgefield, South Carolina, on March 16, 1826. He was the son of Stephen and Elizabeth Garrett. His grandfather, Robin Garrett, fought at the Battle of Kings Mountain. James' first wife was Charlotte Clover. They were married on June 15, 1824. She died on December 24, 1824. James and Jane Harriet had a large family. Their children were Mary Neilson, Sally Elizabeth, Joseph David, Elizabeth Elvira, William Neilson, Lottie, Hattie, James, Foster, Kate, Charles Thomas, Jane Harriett, and Stephen Robert.

Their son, Major William Neilson Garrett, fought in the Civil War. He married Joella Foster. James and Jane Harriett had a stage stand about two miles below Warm Springs on the Drovers Road, located along the French Broad River. A ferry operated across it in 1872. It is listed in the U. S. CONTURE OF MAPS as Love's Ferry. The ferry landed a short distance from James' stage stand. Today this road is called Paint Creek Road.

Phillip Hale Neilson, nephew of Jane Harriett, moved to Wolf City, Texas. His daughter, Sara Lewis Hale Neilson, lived there also.

WARM SPRINGS HOTEL,

WARM SPRINGS, MADISON CO., N. C.

J. A. SAMPLE, Manager for Warm Springs Co.

Patton Hotel facing French Broad River

Back view of Patton Hotel. The pond is water from Spring Creek.
(Picture courtesy of Jacqueline Burgin Painter.)

Patton Hotel Bath House
(Photo Asheville Citizen, Feb. 16, 1983)

27

Famous Patton Hotel in Hot Springs was a landmark until it burned in 1884.

Famous Mountain Park Hotel
(Photos, Asheville Citizen-Times)

Picturesque Village

Hot Springs, or Warm Springs as it was called through the 1800's, was known far and wide as a resort where the springs had amazing soothing and curative results. This is what the village looked like in the 1890's. (Photo Asheville Citizen-Times)

The Old Days

A group of tourists lounge on the front porch of the Mountain Park Hotel in Hot Springs in this picture taken in the 1890s. In those days Hot Springs was a major tourist attraction that drew wealthy people from across the country to bathe in tile pools filled by mineral water heated deep in the earth. The Mountain Park was built on the site of the famous old Patton Hotel which was destroyed by fire in 1884.

Colonel James Henry Rumbough

The Drovers Road on the left, railroad on the right.
The drovers, with their noisy processions of livestock, came up this gorge traveling from the grasslands of Kentucky and Tennessee to the markets of the South and East. The historic route, hugging the banks of the French Broad River, was taken over by the railroad in the 1870's; and the Era of the Drovers came to an end. [THE STATE, March 1977]

History 1786-1883
Warm Springs Hotel – Patton Hotel

As early as 1786, it was important that a road be built up the French Broad River Valley, so as to give a closer route to Augusta, Charleston, and other points east. In March, 1786, it was ordered by the County Court of Greene County, Tennessee, that a road be built to Warm Springs. This road was "laid off" and worked by hand. The overseers were appointed for it by the County Court until 1790.

In 1802, a town to be named Spaightville was authorized to be laid out on the northeast side of the French Broad River, opposite or a little above the warm springs. It is not certain that this town existed. The name of Spaightville was chosen in honor of a former governor, Richard Dobbs Spaight. He died about two months before this act was passed in 1802.[3]

There is no evidence to confirm the fact that a town was ever laid out on the northeast side or the south side of the French Broad River. This two-hundred-acre tract of land at this time was owned by Isaac Taylor until 1808. At this time Taylor sold it to William Neilson, Sr.

In Sadie Smathers Patton's, FOUNDATION STONES OF MADISON COUNTY, she writes, "The development of the first hotel in Warm Springs is an interesting one. The stately Warm Springs Hotel was to develop from an Inn." The Inn was owned by William Neilson, Sr. He probably named the settlement Warm Springs, as he was the first postmaster.

Phillip Hale Neilson, son of William Neilson, Jr., inherited the Inn from his father. He sold the property in 1829 to Green K. Cessna. (Buncombe County Deed Book 16, pp. 74-75.)

Since the Buncombe Turnpike linked Tennessee and North Carolina together, this Stage and Drovers Road ran directly along the water's edge of the French Broad River, nearly the entire distance. Warm Springs was an ideal place for a profitable business. Neilson took care of the horses, wagons, and coaches, as well as the people.

In John Preston Arthur's HISTORY OF WESTERN NORTH CAROLINA (1730-1913), he writes, "his Inn was used during the days of the Drovers. Bishop Francis Asbury, the first Methodist Bishop in America, recorded visiting the Neilson's. According to his diary, the Inn was a regular stopping place. Asbury writes, "on Monday we came off in

---

[3] Powell, William, THE NORTH CAROLINA GAZETTER. University of North Carolina. Chapel Hill Press, 1986, p. 468.

[4] Published by Edward Buncombe Chapter of D. A. R. of Asheville, N.C. Edward and Broughton Printing Co., Raleigh N.C. 1914, p. 491.

earnest, refreshed ourselves at Isaiah Harrison's and continued on to the Paint Mountains, passing the gaps newly made, which makes the road down Paint Creek much better. I lodged with Mr. Neilson, who treated me like a minister, a Christian, and a Gentleman." [4]

The Patton Brothers, James W. and John E.'s, family migrated from County Derry, Ireland, to America. They were great landholders in Asheville, North Carolina. Patton Avenue was named for them. There is little recorded history about the Patton Hotel at Warm Springs, therefore, one has to rely on the people who recorded their visits to the hotel or others who dug deep enough to find any information.

The Patton Brothers bought the Inn and Warm Springs property from Joseph L. Chunn, wife Catherine, and Green K. Cessna on December 6, 1831. (Buncombe County Deed Book 16, pp. 413-414.)

The stately Warm Springs Hotel of three stories was built of white brick. It is common knowledge that the thirteen columns on the porch facing the river represented the thirteen original colonies, and was sometimes referred to as the White House.

Sadie S. Patton's HOT SPRINGS, FAMOUS SINCE 1778, relates that the main part of the hotel, along with the stables, were destroyed by fire in 1838. The fire was caused by an explosion in the boiler room. The structure was rebuilt at a great expense to the owners. The resort was reopened on July 1, 1839. The bridge crossing the river was rebuilt at the same time.

Charles Lanman's HOT SPRINGS —100 YEARS AGO wrote about his trip to Warm Springs in 1848.

> Of the springs there are one-half dozen, but the largest is covered with a house which is divided into two equal apartments. The temperature of the water is 105 degrees. As a beverage it is quite palatable. The Warm Springs are annually visited by a large number of fashionable and sickly people from all the Southern States. The principal building is of brick and the ballroom is two hundred feet long. The hotel has accommodations for two hundred fifty people. There is music and dancing, bowling, bathing, riding, and fishing. [5]

Certainly the recuperative powers of the Warm Springs and the beautiful mountain scenery were the main drawing cards.

In Mary Ellen Wolcott's article, "Zeb Vance Once Clerked In Hotel at Hot Springs," she states, "a number of persons well known in North Carolina history were involved in the establishment and growth of the Warm Springs Hotel. Billy Vance managed the hotel when it was a regular stagecoach stop. A young relative, Zebulon Vance, served as a clerk at this time, later he became Civil War governor. The name of the hotel was changed from Warm Springs to Patton."

---

[5] Lanman, Charles, "Hot Springs—100 Years Ago," THE STATE, March 26, 1955.

Sally Royce Weir wrote about one of the favorite amusements for the guests at the hotel was to start before daylight, riding on horseback to the top of Rich Mountain to see the sunrise. Then go down to the home of Major Broyles at the foot of the mountain for breakfast. Afterwards, one of Major Broyles' Negroes, whose name was Mose, would take the visitors to see the cave. This cave was located near the home of his son-in-law. It has never been fully explored. It is supposed to be three miles long with caverns and streams of water. The old Major was a veteran of the Mexican War. He married a daughter of Colonel Nash, for whom the city of Nashville, Tennessee, was named. Rich Mountain belonged to the Major. He named the high peak Rich because the soil was so fertile.

Wade Hampton built a summer cottage near the springs facing the river. This cottage was just a short distance from the hotel. The bricks for the cottage were brought over from England as a "ballast" in a ship destined for Charleston, South Carolina. They were delivered to Warm Springs by ox cart. This home was destroyed in 1975.

As early as 1783, Warm Springs was considered to be a part of Greene County. According to an old land grant, it was still Greene County in 1790. Buncombe County was formed in 1791. This included Warm Springs. Sixty years later, on January 27, 1851, Madison County was formed. Warm Springs was then a part of Madison County.

James Henry Rumbough

James Rumbough house
Greeneville, Tennessee. (Courtesy of Richard Harrison Doughty)

Colonel James Henry Rumbough

Carolyn (Carrie) Powell Rumbough

Front view of Colonel J. H. Rumbough's home
Hot Springs, North Carolina

Rumbough – Civil War

Mr. Jacob Rumbough was a railroad constructor. He was from Woodstock, Virginia. He supervised the building of the railroad from Lynchburg, Virginia, down the Shenandoah Valley to Greeneville, Tennessee. The method that was used during those days to build a railroad was a contractor would bid on a number of miles and he was responsible for hiring the help and building the railroad. Therefore, the railroad was built a number of miles at a time.

Mr. Rumbough's contract expired in Greeneville, Tennessee, where he decided to live. His son, James Henry, bought a home there June 28, 1858, on South Irish Street, from the Drake Estate for $2000. (Greene County Deed Book 31, pp. 424-425.) The small frame house in the rear garden was a black servant's quarters. Her name was "Mammy Rachel."

Rumbough was born October 19, 1791. He was a very tall man, about six feet, and wore a full beard. Besides being a builder, he liked to read the Bible and fish. He married Ann Danridge Southerland on November 25, 1828. She was a relative of Martha Washington. They had ten children. Mrs. Rumbough died December 3, 1869, and is buried at the Old Harmony Cemetery in Greeneville, Tennessee. After Mrs. Rumbough's death, her husband came to Warm Springs to live with his son, James Henry. Mammy Rachel came also and lived to be 113 years of age. Rumbough died July 27, 1875.

Their son, James Henry, worked with his father from the early age of fourteen. He saved his money, enough to buy and operate a stagecoach line from Greeneville, Tennessee, by way of Warm Springs to Greenville, South Carolina. He was born July 21, 1832. He was a good manager and a very industrious man. He liked adventure and wanted to help open up the country by stagecoach as his father had done by railroad. He married Carolyn Turpin Powell, who was born August 15, 1837. They were married December 12, 1854, at the Saint James Episcopal Church in Greeneville, Tennessee.

Carolyn (Carrie) was the daughter of Joseph Powell, a Federal Circuit Judge. In 1865 he was appointed by President Andrew Johnson as minister to the Falkland Islands. He was a native of Anderson, South Carolina. He was the only member of the South Carolina legislature to vote against secession from the Union.

There was so much anger and hostility that he feared for his family. He decided to move to Greeneville, Tennessee, which was a Union town. He set up his law office there.

James Henry and wife, Carrie, lived about ten years in Greeneville, Tennessee. Their four children were Mary Lee (Bonnie), Kate Mae (Bessie), Henry Thomas, and James Edwin. Mr. Rumbough settled his wife and children near Warm Springs as a safe place from the inevitable war. The farm, located near the Rich Mountain Road, was called the Courtland Farm. Mr. Rumbough stayed busy managing the stagecoach line. Tom Good was one of his drivers. The farm was so isolated, Carrie and her children only stayed a short time before moving back to Greeneville.

Rumbough did not have strong feelings about the war. He did not own a plantation or slaves. His relationship with his in-laws was very good, although they were for the Union. He, being from Virginia, decided to join the Confederacy like Robert E. Lee. It was to his advantage because his stage line ran most of the way through Confederate territory.

He was interested in purchasing the Patton Hotel property in order to get his family out of Greeneville. He knew that he was going to join the army and he did not know if he would survive. He felt that Warm Springs was a safer place to leave them. He moved his family to the Wade Hampton cottage near the Patton Hotel in 1862. The property at this time was owned by Joseph A. McDowell of Madison County.

Rumbough had a formal education and had good leadership ability. He left his family to serve in the Quartermaster Department of the Confederate Army and was commissioned as a Colonel.

Rumbough's son-in-law, Beverly Hill, a young man when the Civil War began, attained the rank of Major in the Confederate Army. He was Commandant at Libby Prison until he was appointed to the staff of General Jeb Stuart. While serving with that great calvary leader during the Gettysburg campaign, he tried to water his horse in the Susquechanna River at Five Forks, where he was wounded. He sheathed his sword at Appomattox and never regretted that the Southern cause was lost, and that we now have a union of states, a union of hearts, and union of hands.

Major Hill was the first mayor of Hot Springs. He served three terms as mayor.

There must have been an agreement between Rumbough and Joseph A. McDowell because Carrie remained living in the Wade Hampton cottage and took over the management of the hotel. Since it was too dangerous to travel, business was slow at this time.

Captain Kirk and his renegades were traveling all through the mountains.

Carrie was a lovely lady with a slender figure and a handsome face. She had a beautiful complexion and natural curly hair, which she kept in a neat style. She was gifted with a brave pioneer spirit and was well trained in all social graces.

During this time she burned the bridge over the French Broad River to prevent an invasion of the bushwhackers or the Union Army. She was afraid they would take her horse. She had the floor taken up in her parlor in order to keep the horse in the house. When the Union Army arrived, one soldier did try to take her horse, but Carrie kept her arms around the horse's neck. An officer intervened and said, "She is a gallant lady. She loves her horse so much, we will let her keep it."

A skirmish was fought at Cuffey Field Ford, located above the second Spring Creek bridge near the creek. Another was fought on the hotel grounds. The ones who lost their lives were buried in a place called the Upper Lawn. Mrs. Elizabeth R. Dotterer told a very touching story about a young Union soldier with golden curly hair, who died in her grandmother's (Carrie Rumbough) arms. Carrie cut off a lock of his hair and sent it to his mother. Although they never met, they corresponded for a very long time.

Colonel Rumbough was taken prisoner near the end of the war near Knoxville, Tennessee. Since his wife's family (Joseph Powell, his father-in-law, was a lawyer in Greeneville, Tennessee) were for the Union, she was permitted to go through the lines. He was released to her after a promise not to take any part in the war. They came back to Warm Springs and the Colonel took over the management of the Patton Hotel. They had four more children, Ann Dandridge, Carolyn Powell, John Charles, and Sara Keyes.

Due to a lack of medicine during the Civil War, the South had to use Indian remedies when they were available. Berries from the dogwood tree were substituted for quinine. They contain the same properties as the cinchona and Peruvian bark. A soothing cordial for dysentery was made from blackberry roots, although ripe persimmons when made into a cordial are thought to be superior to blackberry roots. An extract from the bark of wild cherry, dogwood, poplar, and wahoo trees was used for chills. A tea from wild cherry bark was used for yellow jaundice. A syrup made with leaves and roots of the mullein plant was used for coughs and lung disease. A syrup made from wild cherry bark was also used. Castor bean plant was used for making castor oil. Poppies were grown for opium, from which laudanum was created.

Bicarbonate of soda was found in the ashes of corn cobs. These ashes contain the alkaline properties essential for raising dough. Red corn cobs were better than white for they were thought to contain more carbonate of soda. Okra seed when mature and browned were used as a substitute for coffee, and raspberry leaves were a substitute for tea leaves. Persimmons dried were served for dates. [7]

---

[7] HEROINES OF DIXIE, Katherine M. Jones. Published by Bobbs-Merrill Company, Inc. New York, p. 261.

Town of Hot Springs
November 3, 1891

Seated: Martin McFalls, Alderman; Major Hill, Mayor
Standing: John Daniels, Town Marshall; Bud Lance, Alderman; Newton Lance, Alderman; Major Rollins, Deputy.

Rumbough's Stage Line
Railroad
Patton Hotel Burns

Colonel Rumbough's stage line in Greeneville, Tennessee, July, 1866, originated opposite the former residence of the late President Andrew Johnson. This location could have been on the corner of College and Depot Streets across from the Tailor Shop or on Main Street. His son, Andrew, Jr., married Kate Mae (Bessie), the second oldest daughter of Colonel Rumbough. This stage road from Greeneville ran past the Painted Rock, famous in Indian Legends.

The Buncombe Turnpike was in great need of repair. Colonel Rumbough decided to cut the toll gate down in 1866. The dispute was resolved when the Colonel was allowed to keep the tolls to maintain the road properly.

In Hugh Lefler's HISTORY OF NORTH CAROLINA, he writes that in the spring of 1880, Governor Jarvis persuaded the legislature to sell the state-owned Western North Carolina Railroad, which extended from Wilmington, N.C. to Morganton, N.C. The railroad was encountering much difficulty in crossing the ranges of the Appalachian Mountains, finances being the greatest one. The Governor reported to the assembly that the treasury was unable to maintain the road and complete its construction. He felt the needs of the west would be more quickly met by private capital. Therefore, the state sold the Western North Carolina Railroad to William J. Best of New York, who soon assigned his interest to the Richmond and Danville Holding Company.

The state lost its investment on the road, but Best assumed an $800,000 mortgage. He paid the state $600,000 in cash for its outlay, and agreed to complete the road to the Tennessee line by 1881. This road, which became a part of the Southern Railway System, was finished to the Tennessee line by 1882.

John Preston Arthur's WESTERN NORTH CAROLINA writes about the railroad. It was the first railroad ever built to go through the southern ranges of the Appalachian Mountains. It ran from Asheville, North Carolina, through Warm Springs, to Paint Rock, where it was connected to the East Tennessee Railroad, which was constructed by the Enterprise of the Cincinnati Cumberland Gap and Charleston Company of Tennessee.

The Patton Hotel was destroyed by fire in 1884. The Colonel and his family were living at their "Rutland" home, although he still managed the hotel. He thought it was better to rear his children in a private home rather than in a hotel. He sold the hotel property to a group of northern businessmen, who called themselves The Southern Improvement Company. They built the famous Mountain Park Hotel in 1886. This new hotel faced the railroad. They changed the name of the town from Warm Springs to Hot Springs, which was incorporated on November 3, 1891.

The Southern Improvement Company rejected the Laurel River and Hot Springs Railroad Company, which operated a narrow-gauged railroad from the town of Hot Springs up the mountain to Laurel River, which is Highway 25-70 today. This railroad was used for hauling timber to Hot Springs, where it could be transferred to the Southern Railway for shipment.

The Southern Improvement Company notified the officers of the Laurel River and Hot Springs Railroad Company that by reason of discontinuance of working and running cars over their roadbed, through their lands, that their company had forfeited the right of way. They were trespassers and would have to remove tracks, trestles, and ties from their lands or the said company would take possession of it. They complied with the order, but it was a sorry sight to see, demolishing a line of railroad that was expected to be a great advantage to Hot Springs and Madison County.

The Lobby

The Hotel

Hot Springs, N.C., Mountain Par...

48

Mountain Park Hotel Bath House, Hot Springs, N.C.

Swimming Pool

Bath House entrance and drinking spring

Dairy of Mountain Park Hotel

Mountain Park Hotel
Wana Luna Golf Course

First Golf Club in this area on the grounds of
The Mountain Park Hotel — February, 1895.
(Photos from Pack Memorial Library Collection.)

Wana Luna Club House

Mr. and Mrs. William Baker on left (parents of Miss Peggy).

Mountain Park Hotel
Failure of Mountain Park

The Mountain Park Hotel was built on a hundred-acre park. It was built in the Gothic style, with four corner towers, the front being four stories high. It contained two hundred bedrooms, all of which were well lighted by gas and heated by steam. Some of the rooms had open fireplaces and quite a number were EN SUITE. The lobby was home-like with its deep old-fashioned open fireplace. There was also a hydraulic elevator.

The hotel was famous for its gay social life as well as the curative values of the springs. There were many varieties of amusements. These amusements included bowling alleys, billiard rooms, tennis courts, swimming pool, quoits (horseshoes), riding stables, golf course, boating, target shooting, croquet, mountain climbing, music room, gymnasium, amateur theatricals, and an orchestra that played every evening in the large ballroom.

Hattie's Park, located above Lover's Leap, was a favorite place to picnic. Above Hattie's Park is a large rock called Peter's Rock. This was also a good place for fishing beside the French Broad River.

The legend about this rock is about an old man named Peter, who is said to have fallen from it years before the Civil War while coon hunting. Fortunately, he recovered.

Dr. W. F. Ross, M.D., was resident physician at the Mountain Park Hotel for three years. He recommended the hotel as a place for anyone who was overworked and in need of rest, as well as for the ones who were pleasure seekers.

There was over one thousand feet of verandahs, including one hundred twenty-five feet with glass sun parlors. This provided one-fifth of a mile connected walk under cover for rainy days. The Wana Luna golf course was beautifully located in the hotel park along the French Broad River. It was a nine-hole course, twenty-nine hundred yards around. A golf tournament was open to all the guests.

The large hotel dining room would accommodate about three hundred guests. All the waiters were black men. They wore tuxedos and white gloves. They had to stand in line for inspection every day. Joe Coleman was head waiter. His wife was a cleaning maid. She later taught school at the black Methodist Church at Hot Springs. Uncle Simon Little was a private waiter at the Rumbough family table.

The large bathing house was divided into sixteen separate pools, nine feet long by six feet wide, and four to five feet deep. Each pool was floored and lined with marble. The stairs were also marble. The hot water bubbled up from the floor of the pool at a temperature of ninety-six degrees to one hundred-four degrees. Each bath was provided with a dressing and resting room. Each resting room contained a cot so the bather, wrapped up in a blanket, could recline.

Elegant rooms had been fitted up in the hotel with large marble bathing pools and porcelain tubs into which the water was pumped directly from the hot springs, with all appliances for giving medical treatments. Professor Victor Sherwald was in charge of all bathing departments and Dr. E. G. Peck was the resident physician for several years.

The water from other springs had been walled into a swimming pool, one hundred feet in length by thirty feet in breadth, with a pure gravel bottom. A building had been built with a canopy over the pool which contained individual dressing rooms. No offensive, contagious, malignant, or tubercular-diseased persons were admitted to the baths. They maintained no surgical ward, but provided facilities for regaining health after operations and illnesses.

Two famous people visited the hotel. William Sydney Porter (O. Henry) and his second wife, Sara Lindsay Coleman, spent their honeymoon there. Miss Frances Fisher of Salisbury, North Carolina, who wrote under the pen name Christian Reed, visited during the summer of 1875. She wrote a novel, THE LAND OF THE SKY. It was she who gave Asheville thé famous name "Land of the Sky." She died in 1920.

Another prominent person who came to visit the hotel was the Honorable John M. Francis. He was the founder and senior proprietor of the TROY TIMES newspaper from Troy, New York.

Two other interesting people who lived at Hot Springs for a while were Mrs. Royce and her daughter, Sally Royce Weir. They had a unique house built on the mountain opposite the warm springs, overlooking the French Broad River. The house was designed by one of the women. The architecture of the house was peculiar. Men did the heavy work, but much of the building of the house was performed by the women. A door that was thought to be a china cabinet was an enclosed secret stairway.

The ladies spent a lot of time having wells dug, trying to find hot water. It was very dangerous for a stranger to walk on their property, as one never knew if one would fall into a well. They named their place "The Tempest." Mrs. Weir was an author. She recorded some old legends that were published by the press of S. B. Newman of Knoxville, Tennessee, in 1906.

Failure of the Mountain Park Hotel

The Southern Improvement Company failed to make a success of the hotel. It came back into the hands of the Rumbough family, where it remained for more than sixty years. The hotel and town reached its peak of development under the Colonel. He was an expert at hotel management and he knew what appealed to the wealthy. Mr. Steve B. Roberts of Marshall, North Carolina, was one of his managers.

The Colonel grew most of the food for the hotel, also hogs, beef, and chickens. He had large gardens tended by farmers. Mr. McConey was head gardener. He wanted the town to grow, so he bought a sawmill and built several houses that were scattered over the town. He owned a tobacco establishment at 101 Gay Street in Knoxville, Tennessee.

A financier, E. W. Grove, Sr., of Asheville, North Carolina, tried to buy the property. When he found the land was not for sale, he bought the Charles Thomas (Tom) Garrett property. He drilled wells, hoping to find hot water, but he was not successful.

The Colonel operated the hotel until January 2, 1913. He then sold all the property, all household furniture, bath house furniture, and all equipment related to the hotel to his son, James Edwin, and wife, Mattie, for one hundred thousand dollars. (Madison County Deed Book 30, p. 102.)

James Edwin owned a grain and feed store in Asheville, North Carolina. Since business was slow due to the oncoming war, the Colonel continued to operate the hotel for another year. The hotel was then leased to the Seventh Day Adventist Church from Battle Creek, Michigan, for several months. Later the government leased the hotel for the internment of German civilians.

Hotel footbridge over Spring Creek, washed away during the flood on July 12, 1896.

Roof Upended — The roof covering the porch fell during the flood of 1916. This picture, made just after the waters had receded, shows the damage to the hotel.

Flood Damage — This picture was made just after the Mountain Park Hotel was damaged by the flood on July 16, 1916. Note the walls of this section had been destroyed by the raging waters of the French Broad River.

Flood Debris Piles Up Against Bridge

Remnants of a mobile home and other debris from the Nov. 6 flood stacked up against this bridge in Hot Springs. The flotsam impeded the passage of the high water and added to the peril. (Photo by Bob Gessner) CITIZEN-TIMES. NOVEMBER 29, 1977

Floods of 1896, 1916, and 1977

A flood, causing extensive damage, occurred on July 12, 1896. This flood washed away and destroyed the house of George Roland, turned over the home of Mrs. Stone, and swept away all the fences on the bank of Spring Creek. It also destroyed three trestles from under one bridge and undermined the railroad abutment on the east ridge. The hotel footbridge was entirely demolished.

The Mountain Park Hotel was damaged during the flood of July 16, 1916. The walls of one section of the building were badly damaged, as was the roof covering the porch. The water from the French Broad River covered the hotel grounds up to the back of the depot. The guests in the hotel were taken out by boat. When the water receded, wagons were used to transfer them elsewhere.

Elizabeth Rumbough Dotterer recalls seeing the black waiters, who worked at the hotel, climb trees with baskets of food on their arms. She saw the bridge over the French Broad River wash away. She also saw a house with a rocking chair on the porch go down the river. Burder Fowler is another eyewitness who saw the bridge wash away. The river rose so high it backed Spring Creek out of banks. Iowa Melton was standing near the creek when it washed a house down the creek. The front door was open and a lighted lamp was on a table.

A Southern Railway passenger train, Number 11, had to park on a side track near the Spring Creek railroad bridge (commonly called the trestle) for a time until it was safe to proceed to Asheville.

The steel structure bridge that was built by the town of Hot Springs in 1910 over Spring Creek, which replaced a swinging footbridge that was demolished during the flood of 1896, withstood the flood.

The worst flood in sixty-one years roared through Hot Springs on November 6, 1977. The town suffered great damage. Several huge logs washed down Spring Creek and stopped at the bridge. A trailer home washed into the creek behind the logs, causing trees and other debris to stack up against the bridge. Since the water could not pass under the exit, it spread out, flooding all the businesses. Bill Collins' grocery store was a total loss. He never rebuilt it.

Within hours after the water receded, men and women turned out to help. A backhoe, tilted out over the bridge railing, was used to clear flood debris from under the bridge.

Andrew Johnson Junior

Home of Mrs. Mary Stover Brown in Carter County, Tennessee.
(Courtesy of Richard Harrison Doughty)

Wedding Picture of Mr. and Mrs. Andrew Johnson, Jr.
(Miss Bessie Rumbough) November 25, 1875
(Courtesy of Richard Harrison Doughty)

Daniel Bigelow Safford, 1891
Wearing the clothes required when presented to Queen Victoria

Kate Mae (Bessie) Safford, 1891
Ready to meet Queen Victoria, when she was presented at the court of St. James

Loretta, home of Daniel Bigelow and Bessie Safford

Jack Safford, Bessie Rumbough Safford, Natika, the black nanny Mary Henderson

Altar of Loretta Chapel

Loretta Chapel

Bessie Safford (on left) — 1890s.

Katie Mae (Bessie) Rumbough's First Marriage
Bessie R. Johnson's Marriage to Safford

Colonel Rumbough's second daughter, Bessie, married ex-president Andrew Johnson's son, Andrew, Jr. Bessie was eighteen years old when she married Andrew, Jr., who was twenty-three. They were married at Warm Springs at her parent's home, Rutland, which had been built in 1868. She and her sister, Mary Lee (Bonnie), had a double wedding on November 25, 1875. The sisters attended the Georgetown Visitation Convent School in Washington, D.C. The two younger sisters attended Villa Marie in Abington, Virginia.

Andrew, Jr., was thirteen years old when his parents moved to Washington, D.C. He had a liberal education and went into the field of journalism. He operated a printing shop on Main Street, north of the Andrew Johnson homesite in Greeneville, Tennessee. He and Thomas Maloney, a grandson-in-law of Andrew Johnson, edited and published THE GREENEVILLE INTELLIGENCER, a local newspaper that was issued weekly. [8]

Bessie and Andrew, Jr. (sometimes called Frank) were visiting her parents at Hot Springs, when Andrew, Jr., who was on one of his drinking sprees, had to be put in bed upstairs. A black servant was stationed at his door in the hall to make sure that he was safe.

Bessie decided to go to the Mountain Park Hotel where there was dancing to the wonderful music of an orchestra every evening. In the meantime, Andrew, Jr., sobered up enough to walk out on the balcony that was connected to his bedroom. He proceeded some way to get down on the ground. He managed to walk to the hotel, where he appeared in the ballroom among the beautifully dressed people in his night shirt. The servant, not knowing that Andrew, Jr., had escaped over the balcony, was sitting by the door sound asleep.

Bessie's nearly four years of turbulent marriage to Andrew, Jr., ended with his death at his sister's home in Carter County, Tennessee, on March 12, 1879.

After Andrew, Jr., died, Bessie was very depressed. She told her parents that she was considering becoming a nun. Her father was very distressed. He asked her to come home from Greeneville and he would build her a home at Warm Springs, since she and Andrew did not have a home. He thought living in a new home all her own would lift her spirits. She lived in this home for a time before it burned down.

---

[8] Plaque at President Andrew Johnson's home.

Some of the Colonel's friends in Greeneville were going on a trip to Europe. He encouraged Bessie to go with them. This was about seven years after Andrew died.

Bessie, a young, attractive widow, in 1886 on this voyage to Europe, met and fell in love with a wealthy New York banker, Daniel Bigelow Safford. They were married in London, England, then moved to Paris, France.

Mr. Safford was born April 1, 1830. He was a fine gentleman. He was born and raised in Boston, Massachusetts. He was a member of the Presbyterian Church. His first wife was a Miss Bigelow of Boston. They lived in New York, where he was a member of the firm Lenear and Company. They had three children, one son, George, a daughter, Helen, who never married, and another daughter, who was Mrs. Dan Quintard.

Mrs. Safford was a woman with a great personality. She had brown, naturally curly hair, which she wore in a French style. She was always beautifully dressed.

She and Mr. Safford were presented to Queen Victoria at the court of St. James by Mr. and Mrs. Whitelaw in 1891. The seed pearls on her lace gown, the veil, and heavy train were beautiful. Her train had a weighted cord on the end to keep it straight behind her as she walked into the throne room. She looked like a queen herself. Mr. Safford bought her two pieces of jewelry that had belonged to Empress Eugenia Bonaparte. They traveled extensively in Europe and the Orient. Both of them spoke French fluently.

Their son, Jacque (Jack), was born in France on February 2, 1888. The family came back to the states to the Safford's beautiful estate on Ridge Drive in White Plains, New York. Their daughter, Natika, was born there.

Safford's son, George, by his first wife, owned a seat on the New York Stock Exchange, where he lost many thousands of dollars. This was the beginning of the trying times of the 1890's. Their estate in White Plains was sold to Gedney Farms Hotel Company. The Saffords moved to Hot Springs. Loretta, a beautiful brick French chateau style home, had been built to replace a former one which had burned.

Their home was one of the show places in North Carolina. It contained many rare antique furnishings acquired on their journeys abroad. Velvet drapes, china, and silverware were just a few of the furnishings. The big hall, about the size of a small auditorium, had a black life-size bull dog that looked like he might be there to guard the house. The big hall had four large carved wooden pillars in the center. This is where Mrs. Safford lay in state before her funeral. The hall also had two large fireplaces about five feet wide, with black marble mantels with veins of green running through the black. The rest of the house had five fireplaces that were smaller, with white marble mantels.

To the right of this hall was a music room, which included a baby grand piano. Near the music room was a winding stairway, with a large dial overhead of many colors of glass. In all, the house had fifteen rooms, five baths, plus the big hall and a conservatory.

The Saxe room was a guest room. It had a beautiful carved bed, bureau, chiffonier, and chairs, all imported from France. The conservatory was a large room. One side was all glass, which faced the morning sun. Mrs. Safford kept her ferns and flowers there. She would serve meals in the conservatory instead of the big hall. The hall was only used for special occasions.

The fifty-three-acre estate had an orchard consisting of apple, pear, and cherry trees, and a vineyard with many varieties of grapes. She owned two horses, Lola and Dickie. Dickie was her favorite that she rode until she was about seventy years old. Dickie died in the early 1940's. She had a large number of pigeons in her pigeon house, with a bird bath nearby. The entrance to the rose garden had two life-size statues on either side of the wrought iron gate. These were imported from France. There were many blooming shrubs and bulbs growing around the grounds.

Henry Thomas Rumbough, son of the Colonel, made a gift of land for a church and rectory in Warm Springs on August 10, 1885. Saint John's Catholic Church was a mission of St. Lawrence Catholic Church of Asheville, North Carolina. It was completed between 1886-1889. The church was built of wood under the direction of Father Mark Gross. Since Mrs. Safford was the only Catholic in Madison County after the Dougherty family moved away, she feared someone would vandalize the church. She received permission from Bishop Leo Haid, O.S.B., to transfer all the furnishings of the older church to a beautiful, small, grayish Gothic stone chapel that was attached to the northwest corner of her house in 1905-1906. All the windows were beautiful stained glass. She named the Chapel "Our Lady of Loretta."

The Saffords seemed very happy in their new home. Mr. Philapo, an Italian, was the all-round handyman. He was caretaker of all the property. He helped take care of Mr. Safford, which included taking him to church on Sunday in his surrey with a fringe on top.

Their son, Jacque (Jack), contracted typhoid fever and died on December 26, 1913, at the age of twenty-four.

Mrs. Safford had an artist from New York paint a large canvas of John the Baptist sitting on a rock with a staff in his hand. At the top of the staff was a banner with the words "Behold the Lamb of God." At his side stood a lamb. This painting was pasted to the sloping wall over the altar. The face of John the Baptist was her son Jack's face.

Jean Douglas Garrett
Daughter of Charles Thomas Garrett

The Garretts

The Safford's daughter, Natika, was a lovely girl. A French governess was hired to teach her, but later on she attended St. Genevive of the Pines, a school for girls in Asheville, North Carolina, and one year at Ashley Hall, a women's college at Charleston, South Carolina. She was the granddaughter of Colonel Rumbough.

Natika married Robert Lewis Garrett, son of Charles Thomas (Tom) Garrett and Mary Link. Garrett owned property on the north side of the French Broad River, which was originally owned by his grandfather, William Neilson, Sr. The Garrett House is believed to be the Neilson House. It was a two-story, five-room hewn log house put together with wooden pegs, which had been covered over with clapboards sometime later. Another large two-story, four-room house had been attached to the old house at a later date. There was also a large hewn log smoke house. The lawn was partially surrounded by a paling fence. The walkway to the house was lined with a boxwood hedge. There were many flowering bulbs, one-half acre of flowers, and a vegetable garden. This landscaping was planned like Neilson Sr.'s home in Scotland, which was called "Pleasant Banks."

When this house became a stagestop, it was referred to as the Garrett Inn. The Drovers and Stage Road ran through this property near the Garrett gate on its way to Tennessee. Thomas (Tom) had a blacksmith shop, which was useful for repairing wagons, stagecoaches, shoeing horses, and repairing saddles. He owned several slaves who helped till the land. He had extra help from the farmers who worked for him.

He and Mary had seven children. The children were James Henry Link, Albert Sidney, Charles Thomas, Jr., William Neilson, Kate Comfort, Jean Douglas, and Robert Lewis.

Garrett and Rumbough had a difference of opinion about the Hot Springs. It was reported from Hot Springs that while workmen were working on the property of Tom Garrett on which anthracite coal was discovered, they struck a vein of hot water. This vein of water was supposed to be the one that supplied water to the Mountain Park Hotel. However, it was said that pipes would be laid and the water would be conducted to the hotel without trouble.

Colonel Rumbough said, "The report is in error. I am able to speak authoritatively, by reason of many years of experience and familiarity, that the hot springs supply does not come from the east side of the river but from the very bowels of the earth." [9]

This must have caused a hard feeling between the two, because Colonel Rumbough made the remark, "I may live to eat the goose that picked the grass on old Tom's grave." When he was told about Garrett's death, he said, "Good, good." These two must have

---

[9] Rumbough, Henry Thomas, SCRAPBOOK

been surprised when Garrett's son, Robert, married the Colonel's granddaughter, Natika.

Colonel Rumbough died May 10, 1924, at the age of ninety-two. He was . . . eulogized as being a pioneer resident of Western North Carolina. His activities belonged to the picturesque time of the stagecoach line from Hot Springs to Greenville, South Carolina, by way of Asheville, North Carolina.

At Hot Springs, Colonel Rumbough established one of the most popular summer resorts in the Southern Appalachians, a place that became the home of the South Carolina planters and vacationers from all the Southern states. Hot Springs was famous for its hospitality under Colonel Rumbough's administration and played a notable part in making this mountain region better known throughout the United States. Colonel Rumbough was a splendid type of Southern gentleman, proud of the Southern traditions, and a man of initiative and foresight. Colonel Rumbough was one of the builders of the new Western North Carolina, and, as such, his name will long be remembered. [10]

---

[10] Rumbough, Henry Thomas, SCRAPBOOK.

Hot Springs
It's steeped in military history

General Wade Hampton's cottage
(Photo Asheville Citizen-Times)

Picture of Prisoners

This picture, made by Mrs. Charles T. Rhyne, Sr., appeared in the November 18, 1917, issue of The New York Times. The picture shows the German prisoners "enjoying" the spacious lawn of the Mountain Park Hotel at Hot Springs.

World War I German prison camp

A group of German prisoners of war (World War I)
(Photos Asheville Citizen-Times)

Prisoner walking on hotel grounds

German Band
(Photo Asheville Citizen-Times)

German Village
This attractive village was constructed by scrap lumber and driftwood
near the French Broad River.

Carefully Landscaped
The builders of this building took time and effort to "landscape" its small area carefully.
Note the fence built of limbs and small trees.

Seclusion Spot
It took many hours of work to construct this shelter, which was a part
of the village constructed by the Germans.

Windmill

Attractive Cottage
This two-story cottage constructed in the village along the French Broad River.

This is another rustic chapel.

Artistic German carved a tree trunk into an alligator's head, along Spring Creek.
(Photo Asheville Citizen-Times)

Chapel in the distance is complete.

Interesting Chapel
The German prisoners constructed this chapel
using scrap lumber and tin cans.
(Photo Asheville Citizen-Times)

Doctor Edward Peck

Welland Arnold Thompson, delivering milk to the German Camp.

Ye Ole Well
Constructed near a bridgeway.
(Asheville Citizen-Times photo)

Guards at the prison camp.

Soldiers' Hut

German Internment

At the beginning of World War I, a large trans-Atlantic German ship, THE VALTERLAND, under the command of Commodore Ruser, with four hundred sixty Germans aboard — all but one hundred were officers, entered a United States port. Another ship, THE KRONPRINCESEEN CECLIE, one of the finest merchant ships afloat, was commanded by Captain Pollack. There were one thousand, five hundred sixty-five seamen aboard. Five hundred thirty-one were officers. These people were detained by the government.

Business at the Mountain Park Hotel at this time was very slow due to the war. James Edwin Rumbough went to Washington, D.C., to make arrangements to lease the hotel to the government to have the Germans interned at Hot Springs. These people were not considered prisoners, but internees. They were not allowed to return to Germany or move freely in the states. Twenty local men took a three-hour elementary examination to qualify as guards. Fifty-four guards were needed. They received a salary of $840 a year.

A second large camp was located on the Upper Lawn of the hotel property. The seamen were separated from the captain and officers. The crew who cooked and cleaned the hotel stayed at the officers' quarters. The seamen lived in seven barrack buildings with double deck beds. These buildings were heated by stoves. The typhoid fever epidemic broke out in the internment camp in the fall of 1918. A large number of the victims were taken to the old government hospital at Kenilworth in Asheville, North Carolina. By the time the disease had been checked, the death toll stood at forty. The last eighteen that did not recover at the hospital were buried at Riverside Cemetery in Asheville. The twenty-two others that died before they could be moved from the camp were buried at Hot Springs in the Odd Fellows Cemetery. They were removed in 1933 or 1934.

One of the victims was the bandmaster and the director of the German Imperial Government Bands, which consisted of thirty-four musicians. The group was on a concert tour in China when Germany became involved in the war. They became stranded in the United States when they sought to return to their homeland by way of America.

The food for the internees cost the government forty-five cents a day per man. Some of the food was rice, curry, apples stewed or baked, rye bread (black bread, which the Germans liked), wheat bread, butter, tea, and coffee.

For recreation they played tennis, German football, cards, chess, reading, and everyone seemed to like smoking. They had a wonderful concert band and would sometimes play on the hotel grounds on Sunday evening.

These men were very artistic and spent many hours of time building a German Village on the hotel grounds. This village was designed by Captain Schlimback. Some of the cottages were just one room and were used for clubhouses. They were built of drift or scrap wood and tin cans, and were landscaped with plots of flowers.

The forty families, who came over with the German men, were allowed to live in Hot Springs. They boarded at different places in town. The wife and daughter of a captain stayed at the Lance Sisters' Boarding House. The interned men were not allowed to see their families except for one hour on Sunday when guards were present.

One wife who boarded at the Sunny Bank Inn owned a collie dog. She would write notes to her husband, which she attached to the dog's collar, then she would walk the dog to the Rumbough house (Rutland), where she would sit on a rock wall overlooking Spring Creek. Her husband would sit on the bank watching for the dog to deliver the note. This way they could communicate. This man was the only German to escape. It is believed that he swam the river. She was put under house arrest for a while. At this time the local guards were exchanged for soldiers.

Reverend Walter E. McBath and his wife were Presbyterian missionaries, who came to Hot Springs after being in Guatamala for fourteen years. Rev. McBath was paymaster at the German camp. He was an excellent photographer. He ordered his own materials and mixed his own chemicals for developing his photographs. Many thanks are owed to the Reverend for the historical pictures of the German Village.

Welland Arnold Thompson from Peckville, Pennsylvania, came south to work at different jobs during the winter months. He was trying to save enough money to get married. He was twenty years old at the time. He and his horse, Dick, delivered milk to the German Camp.

On Armistice Day, November 11, 1918, some of the soldiers who helped guard the enternees celebrated by blowing up the German Village. After the war, the hotel was used as an army hospital for the duration of the lease.

Mrs. Bessie Safford owned a quaint cottage near Spring Creek. Her son, Jack, and nephew, Harry Hill, operated an ice plant there until Jack died of typhoid fever.

This cottage had a long room the length of the house. It had old-fashioned beams overhead without a ceiling, and a huge rock fireplace. Mrs. Safford made a recreation room for the soldiers who were guarding the Germans along with some of the local men. This cottage was called the "Soldiers' Hut." It was used as a chapel after "Our Lady of Loretta" burned in 1951.

Warm Springs, N. C., January, 1920

At seven o'clock this evening, the cry of fire startled the citizens of this usually quiet place, and one hour and forty minutes later the Mountain Park Hotel, which has given this place a national reputation as a summer resort, was in ashes. The hotel was one of the largest in the South. There was nothing saved. The hotel was valued at $150,000, but was insured for $50,000. It was owned by James Edwin Rumbough and wife, Mattie E. Rumbough. Origin of fire unknown. [11]

[11] Rumbough, Henry Thomas, SCRAPBOOK.

Berchmans Hall

Natika as a child in White Plains, New York.

Natika as a teenager.

Natika Safford

Bob and Natika's cabin in the process of being built in 1925.

Bob, on the right, and friend, Hans.

The Barn

The Windmill

Bessie Rumbough Safford
Natika Safford's Marriage
Famous Engineer

After Mrs. Safford lost her husband and her son, she decided to do something to help the people in the Hot Springs area. Her brother, James Edwin, and wife, Mattie E. Rumbough, sold her the hotel property on July 26, 1920, for one hundred dollars. (Madison County Deed Book 38, p. 606.)

A man was operating a brick plant on her property. Since he could not pay his rent, she took brick as payment. She had decided to build a sanitarium. Mr. Crum and Mr. Pruitt were going to manage it for her, but there was a disagreement, and the two gentlemen called it off.

After the plans for a sanitarium failed, Mrs. Safford tried to bring doctors and nurses in to operate it. She invited the Catholic Sisters to operate the baths, but to no avail.

The building was completed by 1925. My father, Burnett Moore, helped with the building and was her caretaker for the last four or more years of her life.

The Missouri Province leased the property for three years. The Jesuit Tertianship Building in Cleveland, Ohio, had burned down. Thirty-seven Tertians, six brothers, and instructors arrived in Hot Springs on September 15, 1926. The Tertians were young Jesuit priests, mostly in their early thirties. They studied and helped out in area churches. They named the sanitarium building Berchmans Hall after St. John Berchmans, patron of altar boys. The Tertians departed to their respective provinces on June 30, 1927. Several Jesuits of the New Orleans Province remained on the property for two more years until their lease expired.

Mrs. Safford was a very generous person. She always tried to help the people who could not help themselves. She kept eight to ten milk cows. My father milked them by hand. She supplied the Jesuits their milk and the home for the elderly at Marshall, North Carolina. Anyone who could not take care of themselves or did not have a family to help them were put in the "County Poor House." Several days before Christmas, Mrs. Safford's cook would bake cakes, cookies, and other goodies for a special treat for the residents at the home.

Mrs. Safford died January 9, 1930. She was seventy-three years old. Her obituary is the following:

Mrs. Bessie Rumbough Safford, wealthy society woman of Hot Springs, North Carolina, was killed by fumes from a gas heater in her room at Tallahassee, Florida, where she was visiting her friends. She was taking a bath when she was overcome by fumes. Before Mr. and Mrs. Peck, who were traveling with her, could rescue her, she was dead. Funeral services were at 2:45 p.m. at the private chapel on the Safford's estate. Burial was in the family cemetery. [12]

Mrs. Safford willed everything to the Jesuits of the New Orleans Province of the Catholic Church.

Her daughter, Natika, was disinherited. Mrs. Safford tried to break up a love affair between Natika and Robert Garrett. She did not approve of him because he was not of the Catholic faith, and she also knew that he would get the benefit of her wealth. Natika left Hot Springs to visit a friend, whose husband was a member of the Tennessee legislature living in Washington, D.C. Robert worked on the railroad long enough to buy a ticket to Washington. They were married there and went to New York to be near her half sister, Helen.

Robert and Natika secured a job as caretakers of an estate. She did not return to Hot Springs for sixteen years.

They decided to go to Wembley, Alberta, Canada, in 1919 or 1920 to homestead a prairie farm out of the wilderness, Number SE 24-.9-70-W6. They built a log cabin. Pioneer furniture was used in the cabin; even bear rugs were used on the floor to keep out the cold.

Natika returned to Hot Springs only after her mother died. Due to the failing health of her mother at the time the will was made, she threatened to go to court to contest the will, but the New Orleans Province compromised by giving Natika all the furniture, personal items, and bank account. She did not want the property.

She remembered a secret drawer in her mother's desk where she kept her valuable jewelry. The diamond tiara was missing. No one knows what happened to it, since Mrs. Safford did not confide her business to her relatives. She could have sold it to help finance the building of the sanitarium.

Natika sold some of the furniture in Hot Springs. The antiques that she did not want were taken by freight to an antique store in Asheville, North Carolina. A train car filled with antiques, which included a grand piano, were shipped to Canada. She also fell heir to a substantial sum of money.

Natika was a beautiful lady. She loved sports such as horseback riding, farming and animals, especially her dogs. She would take her dogs to town with her in the car and buy them ice cream cones. She preferred to live in a log cabin, rather than at her parents' beautiful Loretta Estate.

---

[12] Rumbough, Henry Thomas, SCRAPBOOK.

This inheritance completely changed the Garretts' lifestyle. They bought a truck to haul their wheat, corn, oats, and other produce to Grande Prairie, the nearest town with a railroad. They did a lot of building, which included a log barn, and many other livestock buildings. They raised horses, cattle, pigs, turkeys, and chickens. Slim Russel was manager of their farm.

Robert (Bob) in the early days was an ardent hunter and trapper. He liked to hunt moose. Natika was one of the best gardeners in the Peace River area. She grew different varieties of vegetables and canned food for winter use. Her place looked like British Columbia's Butchart Gardens. She brought some of her plants from the United States to their farm. The inside of her home was equal to the outdoors. Her beautiful plants and her parents' antique furniture, imported from France, added to the beauty of her home. She was an excellent butter maker, which she sold to help with the finances.

At this time, Robert decided that he was tired of farming. He wanted adventure. He went to Alaska to look for gold and was gone for four years or more. It makes one wonder if Natika ever thought about her mother's disapproval of her marriage.

When he returned years later a very sick man, Natika built him a small house down by the Wapiti River, which was about a mile and half from her home. She still loved him dearly. They did not ever live together again, but they did visit each other often.

Natika had to have cancer surgery for the third time. She decided that she would like to move back to Hot Springs near her relatives. She wrote her aunt, Mrs. Sara Baker, of Hot Springs, asking permission to put a trailer on her property, which her caretaker was going to build for her. Mrs. Baker was delighted that Natika wanted to spend her last days with her.

Days and weeks went by. Mrs. Baker kept writing to find out what was wrong, but her letters were never answered or returned. Finally, one day Mrs. Baker met Mr. Eugene Rector on the street in Marshall, North Carolina. Mr. Rector worked at the French Broad Bank. It was he who told her that Natika had died.

Before she died, she gave the baby grand piano to a church in Sexsmith, Alberta. Lora Sieker, who cleaned her house in 1944-1945, said there were very few antiques left.

She died in 1946 at the University Hospital at Edmonton, Alberta. She was cremated and her ashes were buried on the home farm by Hans Sieker, which is about nine miles southwest of Wembley. She and Robert did not have any children.

Robert, who was born in 1894, passed away in 1951. He was also cremated and his ashes were spread on the banks of the Wapiti River at his request. Henry Sieker bought the farm in 1954.

For of all sad words of tongue or pen,
The saddest are these - It might have been.
— John Greenleaf Whittier
(MAUDE MULLER)

MIKE O'CONNOR

Mike O'Connor, engineer for Southern Railway, whose route was between Asheville, North Carolina, and Knoxville, Tennessee, was engineer of the Carolina Special, which passed over Spring Creek near Berchmans Hall about 9:30 or 10:00 A.M. From this point, he could see the sanctuary light burning in the chapel. He would blow the engine's whistle and tip his hat in honor of the Blessed Sacrament.

MIKE O'CONNOR'S WHISTLE STILLED
FAMOUS ENGINEER OF SOUTHERN RAILWAY DIES OF STROKE

The mournful melody which only the hand of Mike O'Connor could draw from his special locomotive whistle on the Southern Railway will know its master no more. O'Connor, engineer on the Carolina Special, for many years and with the Southern forty-five years, died at his home. He was sixty-two years old. O'Connor's locomotive was his special pride, and only he was allowed to operate it. A few years ago the railroad honored him on Saint Patrick's Day by presenting a silver nameplate for the green engine with shamrocks embossed on the side. The whistle from which he drew the peculiar notes was his own property, a gift from O. E. Housholder, Southern Railway machinist, who made it himself. Altho O'Connor's friends heard the notes of the whistle with pleasure, other folks were known to shiver with dread as the lonesome tones came through the air. [13]

At one time, six passenger trains passed through Hot Springs every day. The train numbers were 11, 12, 101, 102, 27, and 28. Number 27 and 28 were called the Carolina Special, as they were the only two trains that had a pullman car and diner. Three of these trains were east-bound and three northwest-bound.

Depot agents have been David Gardner, Charlie Burgin, Roy C. Mays, R. C. Kirby and John Lewis Moore. These men worked for the railroad until they retired.

Hot Springs also had Greyhound bus service. Six east-bound and six northwest passed through daily. After I-40 highway was built, the Greyhound Bus service ceased coming through Hot Springs.

Mike O'Connor

---

[13] Rumbough, Henry Thomas, SCRAPBOOK.

COMPANY
407
N. C. 4-7

HOT SPRINGS,
NORTH CAROLINA

EMMETT HAROLD CLEMENTS
1st Lieut., FA-Res.
COMPANY COMMANDER

CLARENCE G. PHIFER
EDUCATIONAL ADVISER

BERNARD JAFFE
1st Lieut., Med-Res.
CAMP SURGEON

102

Camp Life

Class in First Aid

Illustrated Class in Current Events

Road Bank Mulching

Construction of Machine Shop

Road Maintenance

Line-up for Chow

Road Maintenance

Projects of Woodworking Class

Boxing Match

String Band

Retreat

Newton Lance Ice Plant and Sawmill

Hot Springs Electric Power Plant

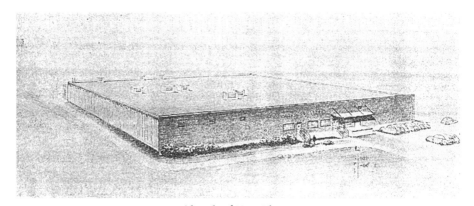

Sketch of New Plant
at Hot Springs for Goodall-Sanford, Inc.

Hot Springs Men's Civic Club

Members were: Alford Maney, Bill Whitten, Rev. S. V. Arthur, Mr. Feltdmose, "Doc" Sumerel, R. C. Kirby, Frank Moore, Rev. Andrew V. Graves, Kenneth Burgin, Bon White, Tom Bruce, Bill Collins, Opie Grubbs, Rex Corn, Glenn Brooks, E. R. Tweed, Mr. Luntsford, Mr. Moser, Mr. Sherouse, Charlie Schaffer, and Jobie Henderson.

*Dotted line shows the approximate boundaries of the site of the Goodall-Sanford,
Inc., plant in Hot Springs.* — Citizen Aerial Photo–Ball

Leaders in the Movement to bring Goodall-Sanford, Inc., to Hot Springs:
Front row (L to R): Mrs. Harry Dotterer, Bill Whitten, Aubrey Ramsey, C. G. Schaffer, Fred Moore,
W. Collins, Frank Moore, R. C. Kirby, C. V. Arthur, Craig Ramsey, Burlin Haney, O. Ramsey and
F. C. Fowler.
Back Row: J. B. Tweed, Harry Dotterer, Henry Plemmons, Doc Sumerel, Cecil Wright, O. W.
Woody, Kenneth Burgin, Tom Bruce, Morris Buquo, Swann Huff, Huffman Lunsford and J. R.
Henderson. — Citizen Photo–Glenn

Prince Garner, Hot Springs' first barber.

Hot Springs' Ball Team during the 1930's
Standing, left to right: D. G. Church, Kenneth Burgin, Ed Runnion, Bill Collins, Swan Huff, Luke Moore.
Kneeling: Hobart Candler, Bud Paris, Herman Pagett, Frank Moore, Reeves Church, water boy Bill
Whitten.

Hot Springs' Friendship Club

113

C. C. C. Camp
Businesses of Hot Springs

After the Jesuits left, Mr. Harry Hill, nephew of Mrs. Safford, was caretaker of the property for the Catholic Church. A part of Loretta was rented out for apartments and several families lived in apartments at Berchmans Hall. The Upper Lawn was used for a C.C.C. (Civilian Conservation Corp) Camp, Company 407. This company was organized May 27, 1933, at Fort Bragg, North Carolina. They were to operate in the French Broad District in the Pisgah National Forest.

Full-time field work began on June 6, 1933. This consisted of road construction, one hundred miles of foot trails were cleared, especially the Appalachian Trail. One hundred and three miles of telephone line was constructed and thousands of white pine trees were planted. They built a seven-room house, office, and garage for the Ranger of this district. They spent thousands of hours fighting forest fires. Camp life consisted of lessons taught in woodwork, first aid, current events, leader training, and kitchen duty. Recreation was boxing, movies, and their own string band.

The Camp was operated like an army camp. They dressed in uniforms and were trained in calisthenics and marching. They would stand at attention when the bugler would blow reveille once a day when the flag was raised. These two hundred men were getting well trained for the oncoming war.

The first pharmacist in Hot Springs was Andrew C. Tainter. The second was Thomas Jefferson Bruce, and later his son, Tom Bruce. The doctors were Edward Peck, W. Ross and David Kimberly.

There was a lime kiln in Hot Springs before 1872. Marcellus Fagg bought land from the J. J. Gudger family October 9, 1872, that was near the lime cliff. "This property on the west bank of the road was close to where the old lime kiln was located." He bought one hundred sixty acres for $450. (Madison County Deed Book F, pp. 158-159).

Ray and Fagg were partners. They called their company Ray and Fagg Lime Kiln.

There was Barytes Company located near Spring Creek about one mile from Hot Springs. It was destroyed by fire September 8, 1899.

> *This evening at 6:30 o'clock, the boiler room of Barytes Company works was discovered to be on fire, and in a few minutes the entire plant was in a sheet of flames. Within three hours, the works were a mass of ruins. The loss as far as can be ascertained tonight is about sixty-two thousand dollars with only nominal insurance. Robert Woody, chief engineer, and Superin-*

tendent W. P. Perry came near losing their lives in an effort to keep the boilers from exploding. [14]

George C. Buquo leased eight acres, more or less, of land August 7, 1911, from T. F. Malley and wife, Minnie Fagg Malley, for five years, for royalty on all limestone quarried for five cents per ton or 2240 pounds. (Madison County Deed Book 29, pp. 125-26-27.)

Buquo, on February 25, 1914, bought one and one-half acres of land for $75 from Henry Fry, Edward and wife, Hester Fry. (Madison County Deed Book 32, p. 20.) The same day, Buquo bought four and one-half acres more land from the Fry's in the name of G. C. Buquo Lime Company for $450. (Madison County Deed Book 32, p, 21.)

The American Agriculture Chemical Company of Connecticut bought land near this site about one mile northwest of the village of Hot Springs, October 14, 1914, from Charles B. and Mollie Hobbs. (Madison County Deed Book 31, p. 448.) This company did not materialize.

The Buquo Lime Company prospered for many years. Since the location was near the Southern Railway, it was convenient to ship the lime by freight cars. The shipping point was called "Buquo Station." Buquo built a commissary for his employees. George Lippard of Hot Springs was his bookkeeper for about seven years. The plant success caught the attention of A Lime Company in Mascot, Tennessee. They did not like competition; therefore, they bought the Buquo Lime Company and closed it down. Buquo went to work for the Grove Stone and Sand Company near Swannanoa, North Carolina.

There were three brick plants. The Henry Fry Plant was located at Lenoir Bottoms (today Harold Baker's farm). This plant washed away during the 1916 flood. The Hunt-Rhinegar-Jenkins Plant was located near Farry's Branch (Blood River). The Red Shale Brick Company leased property from Henry Fry, Edward N. Fry and wife, Hester. (Madison County Deed Book 32, p. 20.) Bricks were made at this brick plant.

Newton Lance and Sons, Frank, Ted, and Hugh, operated an ice plant near their home on the bank near Spring Creek. They also operated a sawmill near the ice plant. Later they operated a small electrical power plant. Their customers were charged a fee for each light, and the power was cut off at night. This was very infeasible for the customers who wanted a refrigerator. Most of the people at this time owned an icebox. Ice was twenty-five cents for twenty-five pounds. Mr. Warren Davis helped to start a small knitting mill in the upstairs over the ice plant, but this plant was not successful.

George Buquo and Bill Ellerson persuaded Carolina Power Electrical Company of Asheville, North Carolina, to come to Hot Springs and install a better generator plant. This was about 1925. George Rhodes was in charge of the power plant. About 1936,

---

[14] Rumbough, Henry Thomas, SCRAPBOOK.

Carolina Power closed it down and Hot Springs received electrical power directly over the mountain from Asheville.

Jack Heilman operated a sawmill at the West Yard, later operated by J. T. Powell of Canton, North Carolina. Cal Garland of Limestone, Tennessee, operated the same mill for several years.

In the late 1950's, the Hot Springs Hotel closed its doors. Craig Rudisell, Sr., in 1956 built a small Memorial Clinic on the hotel grounds, hoping to get Hot Springs a doctor. The nearest doctor was Dr. David Kimberly, who had an office about six miles away.

The clinic did bring some good doctors: Dr. James R. Milling, M.D., Dr. Norton, M.D., Dr. John Ditunno, and Dr. Robert Blake, M.D. Hot Springs now has a new Health and Dental Clinic, which includes Home Health Care. Governor Jim Hunt came to Hot Springs, July, 1983, to dedicate the facilities to the people of the Hot Springs community.

Reverend Andrew V. Graves, S. J., convinced the Northern Province of Baltimore, Maryland, to buy the fifty-three acres of the Safford property from the Southern New Orleans Province in 1941. They bought the property in 1942.

In 1953 Goodall-Sanford, from Maine, formally announced that they would come to Hot Springs with their textile industry. Reverend Graves signed the papers, selling the Safford property to the Hot Springs Development Corporation on April 22, 1953. It was then leased to Goodall-Sanford. Leaders in the movement to bring the plant to Hot Springs, which included the raising of capital to finance the plant and purchase the property, were Charles E. Mashburn, Marshall attorney; the late Arthur W. Whitehurst, Marshall banker (Citizen's); the late Reverend Z. V. Arthur, who was Hot Springs' mayor; Reverend Andrew V. Graves, S. J., president of Men's Civic Club; J. B. Tweed; Senator Calvin Edney; Representative R. R. Ramsey; aldermen R. C. Kirby, Bill Collins, Frank Moore, and members of the Hot Springs Civic Club.

Goodall-Sanford stayed about three years and was replaced by Pacific Mills, Raeford Division of Burlington Industries, Inc. They operated the plant for about eighteen years and were replaced by Melville Shoe Company (Blue Ridge) for about eight years. The plant has remained closed since Blue Ridge left.

Eventually the Jesuits sold the Mountain Park Hotel property to four businessmen from Marshall, E. R. Tweed, Steve Roberts, A. W. Whitehurst, and Guy Roberts. The name Berchmans Hall was excluded and the building was used as a hotel. It operated under several names: The Spa, Hot Springs Hotel, and Montaqua. Business was profitable for several years. Finally Mr. Craig Rudisell, Sr., of Marshall became the sole owner.

When Hot Springs was a more progressive town over the years, there were a number of businesses. The businesses were:

116

Ebbs Livery
Rowdy Bill Lawson, grocery
Steve Plemmons, grocery and dry good
Nicholson & Erwin Lance, grocery and dry good
Warren Davis Produce
Starlin Ricker's Grocery
Bruce Drug Store
Ebbs and Frisby, hardware
Plemmons and Paris, grocery
Allen's 5 and 10 (located under Tammany Hall)
Abe Long, Joe Lawson, Ed Church, grocery
Peggy and Harry's Cash and Carry, grocery and miscellaneous
Campbell Fowler, grocery
Ira Plemmons and Son, hardware, caskets, and dry goods
Clover Leaf, grocery
Crit and Althea Stamey, fruit stand
Charlie Gowan, grocery
Runnion's Carolina Grocery (later Carolina Grocery)
Ricker's Grocery
Bill Collins Grocery
Tweeds Dry Goods
Bon White's Dry Goods and Furniture
Alfred and James Gentry, furniture and hardware
Schaffer and Wright, dry goods and miscellaneous
Dennis Church, grocery
Ponder and Ponder, hardware, seed, and fertilizer

Over the years there have been several cafes in Hot Springs: Effie Gowan, Sara and Otis McFalls, Dixie, H & L, Burder Fowler's lunch counter (coffee 5¢, plate lunch 35¢, hamburger 15¢, 1/4 pie 10¢), Huffs Restaurant, Trail Cafe and Smokey Mountain Diner.

The boarding houses with meals were: Stone House, Lance House, Martin & Lizzie McFall (later McFee Hotel), Sunny Bank Inn (Mrs. Jane Gentry), Elmer's Inn, and Ira Plemmons' Hotel.

Barbers: The first known one was Prince Garner (black) who worked as a barber on a private railroad car for a Captain McBee, who was supervisor over the Southern Railroad Division. McBee would have his private car parked on a side track and visit the Mountain Park Hotel. Garner was very polite and well-trained with good manners. He married a very lovely girl by the name of Dora. He decided to leave the private railroad car and was employed at the Mountain Park Hotel. He died in 1928, at the age of seventy-two. Other barbers have been Jennings Runnion, Rady Waldroup, Hoke Reeves, and Clyde Huntsinger.

The beauticians were Pauline Church, Mrs. Cheek, Mrs. McClendon, Mrs. Edwards, Vera Buckner Sumerel, Hazel Moore and Judy Khodayar.

The Citizens Bank's employees were Mr. Warren Davis, cashier; Reverend Z. V. Arthur, cashier; Frank Moore, cashier; and Joe Tilson, cashier. The Citizens Bank merged with Wachovia in 1973.

Churches, Schools, and Cemeteries
Haunted Tales
History 1976-1992

The churches of Hot Springs are Baptist, Methodist, Catholic, Presbyterian, and Free Will Baptist. Colonel Rumbough's son, Henry Thomas, gave land to the blacks to build their own church. The whites were invited to attend and some did go when it was convenient on Sunday afternoons. During the week this church was used as a school. After the blacks moved away, except one elderly lady who attended the white Methodist Church, the black church was torn down.

Colonel Rumbough, a Methodist, built an Episcopal Church, Saint John's in 1888. It was built near his home. His wife was an Episcopalian. The guests from the hotel would attend, also the Lance sisters, Sue, Georgia, Fannie, and Mamie. These sisters were famous for their old time way of cooking. This church was also used as a school. About eighteen students attended. Lattie Brooks was one of the students. Miss Callahan from New York was the teacher. The church was torn down about 1953. There is one solitary grave in the churchyard. Clarence Stewart died May 27, 1899. This child and his parents were guests at the Mountain Park Hotel. Since he died from a contagious disease, the parents were not allowed to move him.

There was a good relationship between the blacks and whites in Hot Springs. There was just one incident that created a problem, but it was solved very quickly.

Simon Little (black) helped take care of Colonel Rumbough until the Colonel decided to spend his last days with his son, James Edwin, in Asheville. Little then became custodian at the white school for many years. He was a kind and good man. The adults as well as the children called him "Uncle Simon."

During the Depression, a black widow shared all her farming tools and equipment with a white family, as they did not have any tools with which to farm that year. The Ku Klux Klan in Hot Springs did not bother the blacks. They were prejudiced against the Catholic students who came to Hot Springs to study at Berchmans Hall. They demonstrated by burning a cross and exploding a blast of dynamite across the French Broad River opposite Berchmans Hall.

Other black families that lived in Hot Springs were the Walker (Johnson) family; Dick Bryant family; Right Stokley family; George and Hattie Barnett; Prince and Dora Garner; Anna Nicholas and sons, Jim, Gus, Charlie; Mary Stokley and family; Adken and Bell Brasselton; Jerry and Blanche Huston, children, Willie Mae, Marie, Robert, and Alene; Joe Coleman and family; Luther and Lucille Smith, and daughter, Beatrice; Eugene and Sadie Harris; Coreen Harris; Mont and Alice Gudger; Janie Lyons and husband; Francis and Maggie Stokley; Joe Ann Davis, son, Luther, and daughter, Elvira; Dolf and Jane Bryant; Allie Sisk and son, Henry.

Three black men from Hot Springs, Dick Hutchins, Joe Coleman, and Prince Garner, were chosen to go to a convention that was to be held at Marshall, North Carolina. The white men who went were N. J. Lance, L. J. Sawyer, Thomas and Joe Lawson, H. T. Rumbough, V. D. Davis, Sol Thomas, L. C. Hipps, A. C. Tainter, and Amos Stackhouse. Stackhouse owned a store on the north side of the French Broad River near Sachett Branch.

Hot Springs did not have street signs until the Women's Civic Club had them erected in 1956. This club was active for about two years. The older people, especially Henry Thomas Rumbough, gave names to different sections of town. These names were High Cove, New Town, Scuffletown, and Johnson City.

Recreation at Hot Springs over the years were box suppers, ice cream suppers, and silent movies at the Tammany Hall, which was located above what is now Ponder's Seed and Fertilizer Store. This hall was also a meeting place for the Ku Klux Klan. Years later the high school auditorium was used for movies. The state furnished the movies and Dorland Bell School owned the projector. This way, all the students could join together to enjoy the movie. On special occasions, movies were shown at night for the people of Hot Springs and the surrounding area. Otis Bollinger used an old building near Tammany Hall as a theater, which opened on July 4, 1941, but was damaged by fire on Christmas Day of 1941.

Charles and Louise Schaffer from Jefferson City, Tennessee, came to Hot Springs in 1945. They repaired the building and opened up the Times Theater, which was very successful for many years.

For the ones who wanted to go swimming, there were the Dudley Falls, Spring Creek Falls, Silvermine Pool, and Swirl Hole in Spring Creek, which was also used for baptizing. There were baseball and football games, horseshoe, and talent contests were held for all the people who could play an instrument, sing, or dance. Musical radio groups were brought in to perform at the school auditorium. Some of the groups were the Calahan Brothers, Carl Story and his musicians, J. F. G. Farm Boys from WWNC Radio Station in Asheville. A fee was charged to seen these shows. These groups were sponsored by a class, P. T. A. or other groups who wanted to raise money for a project.

The town had four beer parlors. The proprietors were Tom Russell, Alfred Maney, Charlie Duckett, and Woodrow Gregory. This did not cause a problem because the town had a good policeman, nicknamed "The Black Spider."

The taxi drivers were Bud Ramsey, Huffman Luntsford, Woodrow Gregory, Tom Russell and Fred Anderson.

The Sunshine Club was organized for the women in the early 1940's. Its name was changed June 2, 1950, to the Friendship Club, which is still active. They help with different civic projects in the community.

A group of Hot Springs men organized a Men's Civic Club in 1947. This club was very active until 1957 when they joined the Lions Club. They also had a Gun and Skeet Club. This club usually held a contest every year near Thanksgiving, giving turkeys for prizes.

Hot Springs did not have a library until 1955. Elizabeth Rumbough Dotterer (Miss Peggy) drove a bookmobile, which consisted of a lending library to all parts of Madison County.

The town won two contests in the 1950's, sponsored by the Carolina Power and Light Company of Asheville, North Carolina, called "The Finer Carolina." This $1500 was used to buy a building. The town permitted Miss Peggy to put a library in the back of the building. The front was used as a community center. She was awarded a plaque by the Library Board at Marshall, North Carolina, July, 1984, for sincere appreciation for twenty-nine years of faithful and unselfish service to the Madison County Library.

Katherine Ferguson, an efficient librarian, who worked for five years at the Hot Springs Primary and Elementary School, became librarian for the town, after Miss Peggy retired. She has been working very diligently since 1984.

Looking back through the years, Hot Springs has made many advances in the educational field. The first school in Hot Springs was Dorland Bell Institute, organized by the Reverend Luke Dorland in 1888. It was here that the girls and boys who wanted an education came to learn. The boys lived on a farm called the "Willows," but was later referred to as The Boys Home. It was located about two miles from Hot Springs. Many of the young people, both male and female, came to Dorland from the rural and remote areas of the county, as well as from neighboring Tennessee, to get their education. There have been students who have gone far in life after having graduated from this institution. In later years, other schools were being constructed as public schools, and Dorland Bell closed its doors in 1942.

Even during the time that Dorland Bell was in operation, there was another school formed, which was located on Hill Street. The building was a large four-room house and could care for children from grade one through grade nine. Some of the first teachers at this Hot Springs School were Mrs. Maude Gentry Long, Mrs. Esther Craine Brooks, Reverend Pipes, and Orla Plemmons Joyner. This school began about 1914. Their P. T. A. consisted of 62 members. Lon Brooks was president and Mrs. W. T. Davis was vice-president.

In 1925, the rural schools of the surrounding communities were consolidated with this small four-room school in Hot Springs.

A bid was made on building a large school with four years of high school work. This bid was made on April 13, 1925. A second bid was made on May 4, 1925, by A. B. Moore for $27,990. The new school opened in the fall of 1926 and was known as Hot Springs High School. Students were brought to the high school by bus from Paint Rock,

1927

H.S.H.S. Faculty 1928

Miss Hallum

Miss Hames

Miss Camada '27

Miss Haynes

Mr. Farmer

1928

124

Antioch, Upper and Lower Shutin, Blood River, and the surrounding areas near Hot Springs. The first graduating class of this school was in 1927. In 1946 the twelfth grade was added to the curriculum, extending a student's work to twelve years before graduation. In 1973 a kindergarten was opened for the five-year-old children, adding another year to one's stay in school.

After many years of hard work, Madison High School became a reality. This new consolidated high school was opened in the fall of 1974. This left Hot Springs and the other high schools with grades K through 8. These schools became primary and elementary schools, and all are property of Madison County.

The original Hot Springs High School building, erected in 1925-26 was demolished in 1991. A beautiful new building now stands near the former building site. Spring Creek students also enjoy the beauty and comforts of this new building.

The Unaka School for retarded adults opened in the early 1970's.

Hot Springs has one of the oldest cemeteries in Madison County. The Neilson-Garrett Cemetery was privately owned, although the family allowed others to be buried there. William Neilson, Sr., and his wife, Jane, who died at Warm Springs, are buried there. He was buried in 1832 and Jane in 1816.

The Garrett family buried there are Charles Thomas (Tom) and wife, Mary Link; Tom's second wife, Sallie Frazer; Albert Sidney, James Henry, Charles Thomas, Jr., Children of Charles Thomas and Mary; Elizabeth and Harriett, sisters of Charles Thomas; James R. Garrett and wife, Jane Harriett Neilson, parents of Charles Thomas; William Neilson, Sr., and Jane were grandparents of Charles Thomas.

There are other graves that were marked with a stone. Some of the people were slaves, farm workers, and strangers who were passing through. One was an Englishman. This historical cemetery has been desecrated. Only three tombstones are left. Part of the cemetery has been turned into a barnyard, and land is being tilled over the Garrett family plot of 100 feet by 80 feet, as well as other people who are buried there. At one time this cemetery was a peaceful place with boxwoods and fenced in for privacy.

Other graves have been found near the James Garrett stage stand. One tombstone is all that is legible.

In memory of Benjamin Hourworth
Son of D. C. and E. C. Hourworth
Died August 1, 1825 — age 22 years 8 mo. 6 days

Two people were buried on a hill overlooking Serpentine Road. Mr. Jacob Rumbough, father of Colonel Rumbough, who spent his last days at Warm Springs with his son, was buried there. Later he was moved to Greeneville, Tennessee, where he was buried beside his wife in the Old Harmony Cemetery. The family black servant, Mammy Rachel, was buried there. No one knows if she was ever moved.

There is also an Odd Fellows Cemetery located on the mountain overlooking the Spring Creek Road near the Appalachian Trail.

A town with a haunted house is very interesting. Hot Springs had three — Rutland, Loretta, and Garrett Inn.

Reverend Farnum, an Episcopalian minister, from Asheville, North Carolina, would come to Hot Springs once a month on the Carolina Special (27) for a service at Saint John's Episcopal Church. He always spent the night at Rutland, home of Mrs. Sara Rumbough Baker. This house had twenty rooms, which included a tower room. The third floor had not been used in years. Reverend Farnum slept in one section on the second floor. On this particular night it was very hot, so he left his bedroom door open. During the night he was awakened by a woman standing in his door. The next morning, he said to Mrs. Baker, "I would not have left my door open last night if I had known you were going to have visitors." Mrs. Baker replied, "I did not have visitors. What you saw was the dear departed."

Mrs. Baker's son-in-law, Harry Dotterer, was spending the night alone there. During the night, he heard someone coming down the stairs from the third floor. It sounded like a woman with a long dress with weights. Long ago women wore weights on their dresses. It went tap, tap, tap until it came to the bottom of the stairs. He picked up his pistol and went out into the dark hall. There was no one there. The house was very quiet but his heart was racing.

Different people have heard walking and other unnatural things at the Garrett House and the Safford House (Loretta). The sound of someone walking on the second floor of Loretta down a long hall to the Blue Room, and a man dressed in gray walking down the hill.

The third hotel was destroyed by fire May 29, 1976. A week earlier, on May 22, about 11 p.m., a mysterious fire was discovered in the dining room and back porch. Firemen extinguished the blaze before the flames spread to the main portion of the hotel. On May 29, about 10:45 p.m., flames were discovered again, coming from the hotel. The firemen answered the call immediately. However, for lack of water at the lone fire hydrant near the hotel, it was impossible for firemen to extinguish the fire. The main water line to the fire hydrant had been rusted and falling apart for years. It was reported that most of the rooms on the second floor contained beds and several valuable antiques, including a grand piano. The fire was thought to have been caused by arson.

The hotel was formerly a lovely, furnished place with splendid dining room facilities. Meetings and banquets were frequently held there. It was one of Western North Carolina's most popular and beautiful places to visit and enjoy the warm mineral baths.

Since the 1980's, Hot Springs has been going through a depression, but the future is looking better. A new manufacturing plant plans to open in June 1992, at the old

Meville Shoe Company building. The town has been trying to find an occupant for the building for several years but has been unsuccessful.

The Perfection Gear, Inc., from Asheville, North Carolina, will open a plant at Hot Springs under the name of Madison Manufacturing. They plan to hire one hundred people. Mr. Seth Metcalf will be general manager.

One asset to Hot Springs is that about fifteen hundred hikers from the Appalachian Trail pass through Hot Springs each year. The town's accommodations for these hikers are Elmer's Inn, Duckett House Inn, Alpine Court, and the Brick House. The Jesuits have a Hikers' Hostel. It is also used for Habitat for Humanity groups who help people in need. College students sometimes come during their winter break and help chop wood in the Pisgah National Forest, to be delivered to the poor.

On Highway 209, three miles from Hot Springs, is Rocky Bluff, a government camping and picnic area. It was dedicated on Sunday, April 26, 1965, at 3 p.m. by Roy A. Taylor, United States Representative from the Eleventh District. Ceremonies for the new Post Office were held on Saturday, April 25, 1965, at 2 p.m. Congressman Taylor presented an American flag. The flag ceremonies were conducted by members of the Hot Springs Lions Club. Over a thousand people were present.

There are two other government picnic and camping areas, Murray's Branch, about five miles from Hot Springs, on the Paint Creek Road beside the French Broad River. The people who ride the rafts dock there. Rafting is a very popular sport at Hot Springs during the warm months. Carolina Wilderness Adventure, Inc., Nantahala Outdoor Center, and French Broad Outpost own the rafting businesses. Silvermine campground is located near the raft business office. It is a camping area for groups who want to stay near the town of Hot Springs.

Elizabeth Rumbough Baker Dotterer says, "Yes, there was a silver mine." She has seen a mould owned by an old timer, who lived up Shelton Laurel, who claimed that his ancestors made counterfeit silver dollars, and got the silver from the Silvermine area. Another convincing fact was the arrival of an elderly lady many years ago to the area. She had come to look for the place where her husband and sons had mined silver before the Civil War. They had closed the mine and had gone to fight in the war. The mine has never been rediscovered.

Eugene Hicks, a retired aviator, gave up a profitable aviation service, Colonial Helicopter of Norfolk, Virginia. He and his wife, Ann, moved to Hot Springs in 1990, where he has Madison County roots. The Hicks considered the hotel property a jewel and their great ambition was to own it. After seven years of negotiation, they finally became the owners.

The Jacuzzi tubs are in operation near the bank of the French Broad River. After the use of each tub, the water is drained, the tubs are cleaned and sterilized for use by the next bather. During the busy season, it is necessary to make an appointment. A masseuse, Alberta Benninger, is on call. The time limit for a bath is one hour. The Hicks plan many improvements. The bath house is going to be repaired and a small building is going to replace one that was over a spring which the flood washed away. This spring has an old-fashioned type pump from which one can get a drink of water. The swimming pool, which the flood filled with sand, is to be cleaned out. The Welcome Center has been remodeled and the Hot Springs Resort Campground is under development. This campsite is located on the Upper Lawn, across the Dixie Highway. The Hicks also plan to open the Wana-Luna Golf Course and landscape the land along the French Broad River. A lodge will be built near the hotel site.

Hot Springs (Uma-ooh-de-leg-gee-gah-nuh-go-gutt — Hot Springs in Cherokee) will never be what it was one hundred years ago or Ponce de Leon's "Fountain of Youth," but with a lot of hard work and plenty of ingenuity, it will start bubbling again.

Back to Hot Springs, North Carolina, I'm hankering to go,
to those majestic mountains where the rhododendrons grow.
I love to view the old French Broad and Lover's Leap
as well, and Painted Rock, and hike along the Appalachian Trail.

I would like to dwell in a Haunted House,
but I would live in dread,
less some uninvited ghost would tamper with my bed.
I yearn to hear those old time songs,
and the bloody tales of yore,
I'd like to see old Roaring Fork and Carson Lawson's store.

And the tiny chapel watched o'er by Reverend Graves,
who spoke to us of Peace on Earth, and bade us mend our ways.
Some day I hope I may return to dear old "Mountain View,"
And take my family with me, bidding Indiana Adieu. [15]

---

[15] Written by a guest at Mountain View Tourist Court.

HOT SPRINGS HOTEL AND SANITARIUM
HOT SPRINGS, N. C.

DAYS PROGRAM FOR SANITARIUM GUESTS AND PATIENTS

6:30 A.M.—Morning Shower. Treatment Room.

7:15 A.M.—Breathing Exercises and Calisthenics. Lawn or Gymnasium.

7:40 A.M.—Morning Worship.

8:00 to 9:00 A.M.—Breakfast.

9:15 A.M.—Corrective Gymnastics and Games. Walking and Mountain Climbing.

*9:00 A.M. to 1:00 P.M.—Men's Treatments.

1:00 to 2:00 P.M.—Dinner.

2:00 to 3:00 P.M.—Rest Period.

3:00 P.M.—Corrective and Medical Gymnastics, followed by Games and Folk Dancing.

*3:00 to 6:00 P.M.—Treatments for Women.

*4:00 P.M.—Tennis, Golf, Horseback-riding, Boating and other sports.

6:30 P.M.—Supper.

7:30 P.M.—Marching and Folk Dancing.

*8:00 P.M.—Moving Pictures, Lectures, Concerts, etc.

9:30 P.M.—Rest.

*The foregoing schedule is optional and free to guests except treatments, certain pay entertainments, and some sports as follows:

Tickets for Golf, 50c per day; $2.50 per week; $15.00 per season.

Horseback-riding, $2.50 per day, $1.50 per half day. Row Boats, 25c per hour; $1.00 per day; $3.00 per week. Canoes, 50c per hour; $1.50 per day; $5.00 per week.

Special instructions in all forms of dancing, games and sports at reasonable rates.

The fine athletic grounds are free to guests for tennis and all lawn games and sports.

The Spirit of the Place is to do something Out of Doors every day. We are making it "The Recreation Centre of the South."

(OVER)   36240

NEW YORK—Leave New York on Washington and Southwestern Limited over Pennsylvania Railroad at 4.38 p. m.; arrive Hot Springs 3.30 following afternoon. Through Pullman, Dining, Buffet, Drawing Room and Sleeper service.

ATLANTA—Leave over Southern Railway 7.15 a. m.; arrive Hot Springs 8.05 p. m.

CINCINNATI—Leave over Q. & C. at 8.05 p. m., arriving at Hot Springs 12.45 following noon. Through Pullman, Drawing Room, Buffet and Sleeper service.

CHARLESTON, S. C.—Leave over Southern Railway Carolina Special; arrive Hot Springs 8.05 p. m.

CLEVELAND—Leave over Big Four at 12.35 noon, arriving at Cincinnati at 7.50 p. m. Proceed as directed for Cincinnati above.

MEMPHIS—Leave over Southern Railway at 8 p. m.; arrive at Hot Springs 11.40 following noon. Through Pullman service; or 10.30 a. m. and arrive at Hot Springs 5.30 following morning.

LOUISVILLE—Leave over Southern Railway at 8.10 p. m., arrive at Hot Springs 11.40 a. m. following morning. Or leave over L. & N. 8.30 p. m., arrive at Knoxville 8.15 a. m. and leave at 9.34 a. m., arriving at Springs 12.45 noon.

ST. LOUIS—Leave over Southern Railway 12.04 noon, arrive at Hot Springs 11.40 a. m. Through Pullman service.

NEW ORLEANS—Leave over Q. & C. 7.30 p. m., arrive at Hot Springs 8.05 p. m. following evening. Leave over L. & N. 9.25 a. m., arrive at Hot Springs 3.30 p. m. next day.

HOW TO REACH HOT SPRINGS

JACKSONVILLE—Leave over Southern Railway 9 a. m., arrive Hot Springs 3.30 p. m. following day. Through Pullman, Drawing Room, Buffet and Sleeper service.

Direct connections with Atlanta, Savannah, Augusta, Macon, Birmingham, Mobile, Shreveport, and other principal cities of the South, and all Northern cities.

For further information write to or call on any of the following, who will gladly supply it:

ASHEVILLE, N. C.—J. H. Wood, District Passenger Agent, 60 Patton Ave. R. H. Graham, Ticket Agent, 60 Patton Ave.

AIKEN, S. C.—C. E. Monts, Ticket Agent.

ATLANTA, GA.—James Freeman, District Passenger Agent, 1 Peachtree St.

AUGUSTA, GA.—A. H. Acker, Traveling Passenger Agent, 729 Broad St.

BALTIMORE, MD.—L. H. Burgess, Traveling Passenger Agent, 119 East Baltimore St.

BIRMINGHAM, ALA.—M. H. Bone, District Passenger Agent, Empire Building.

BOSTON, MASS.—Geo. C. Daniels, Passenger Agent, 362 Washington St.

CHARLESTON, S. C.—W. E. McGee, Division Passenger Agent, 217 Meeting St.

CHICAGO, ILL.—Stanton Curtis, Northwestern Passenger Agent, 99 Adams St.

HOUSTON, TEX.—N. A. Vernoy, Traveling Passenger Agent, 207 Main St.

JACKSONVILLE, FLA.—G. R. Pettit, District Passenger Agent, 108 West Bay St.

KANSAS CITY, MO.—Wm. Flannelly, Traveling Passenger Agent, Board of Trade Building.

LEXINGTON, KY.—H. C. King, City Ticket Agent, 111 E. Main St.

LOS ANGELES, CAL.—T. F. Fitzgerald, Traveling Passenger Agent, 207 W. Third St.

MEMPHIS, TENN.—C. E. Stewart, City Passenger and Ticket Agent, The Porter Building, 10 N. Main St.

MOBILE, ALA.—Porter King, City Passenger and Ticket Agent, 84 N. Royal St.

MONTGOMERY, ALA.—Jno. Metcalfe, Traveling Passenger Agent, 9 Commerce St.

NEW ORLEANS, LA.—A. J. Lee, District Passenger Agent, 704 Common St.

NEW YORK, N. Y.—Alex. S. Thweatt, Eastern Passenger Agent, 264 Fifth Ave.

NORFOLK, VA.—F. R. McMillin, Passenger Agent, Monticello Hotel, 95 Grandby St.

OLD POINT COMFORT, VA.—J. N. Smith, Ticket Agent, Chesapeake Line Steamers.

PHILADELPHIA, PA.—C. W. Westbury, District Passenger Agent, 828 Chestnut St.

RICHMOND, VA.—S. E. Burgess, District Passenger Agent, 920 E. Main St. C. C. Shankle, Ticket Agent, 920 E. Main St.

SAVANNAH, GA.—J. S. Bloodworth, City Passenger and Ticket Agent, 141 Bull St.

ST. LOUIS, MO.—T. J. Connell, District Passenger Agent, 719 Olive St. H. J. New, Traveling Passenger Agent, 719 Olive St. J. A. Edwards, City Passenger and Ticket Agent, 719 Olive St. E. E. Gordon, City Ticket Agent.

WASHINGTON, D. C.—L. S. Brown, General Agent, 705 Fifteenth St., N. W.

ANALYSIS

OF THE THERMIC WATERS OF HOT SPRINGS, N.C.

AS CONTAINED IN ONE UNITED STATES STANDARD GALLON

CHLORIDE OF SODIUM	1.0827 GRAINS
CHLORIDE OF POTASSIUM	0.6162 "
SULPHATE OF POTASSA	1.6168 "
SULPHATE OF LIME	20.0416 "
SULPHATE OF MAGNESIA	7.2001 "
BICARBONATE OF AMMONIA	TRACES
BICARBONATE OF IRON	0.1012 GRAINS
BICARBONATE OF LIME	9.0186 "
PHOSPHATE OF SODIUM	TRACES
ALUMINA	0.0385 GRAINS
SILICA	3.1433 "
ORGANIC AND VOLATILE	TRACES
TOTAL	42.8631 GRAINS

ANALYSTS:
C.F.CHANDLER, PH.D.
C.E.PELLEW, E.M.

TEMPERATURE
84°-104°

THESE WATERS HAVE BEEN FOUND TO BE PRACTICALLY A SPECIFIC IN THE CURE OF RHEUMATISM, GOUT, RHEUMATIC GOUT, SCIATICA, JOINT DISEASES, AND ALL TROUBLES ARISING FROM URIC ACID DIA-THESIS.

THEY ARE ESPECIALLY EFFICACIOUS IN THE TREATMENT OF NEURAS THENIA, THE VARIOUS FORMS OF DYSPEPSIA, NERVOUSNESS, INSOMNIA, AND INTESTINAL INDIGESTION; AND ARE OF GREAT BENEFIT IN BRING ING RELIEF TO DIFFERENT CATARRHAL AFFECTIONS, WHETHER OF HEAD. STOMACH, BOWELS OR OTHER PARTS OF THE SYSTEM.

Map showing the French Broad River area with Drover's Road.

Labels on map:
- CARNE CO. TENN.
- § PAINTED ROCK
- FRENCH BROAD RIVER
- JAMES GARRETT STAGE STAND
- RAIL ROAD
- TOM GARRETT INN
- GARRETT FERRY CROSSING
- NEILSON INN
- DROVER'S RD.
- WARM SPRINGS
- FUTURE SITE OF C.C.C.
- LOVER'S LEAP
- RAIL ROAD 1882

MAP BY DOROTHY RISHER   DROVER'S ROAD PRIOR TO 1828 — RAIL ROAD 1882

132

NOTES

1. GEOGRAPHY OF THE AREA
   WILD FLOWERS OF NORTH CAROLINA, William S. Justice and C. Ritchie Bell. University of Chapel Hill Press, 1968, p.141.
   APPALACHIAN TRAIL, U. S. Forest Service Pamphlet.
   THE NAME OF THE FRENCH BROAD RIVER, Elizabeth R. Dotterer.
   Pse-li-co, Charles Lanman, "Hot Springs — 100 Years Ago"
   THE STATE. (March 26, 1955) p. 13.

2. HISTORY 1778
   LEGENDS
   "Warm Springs Discovered," J. G. Ramsey in his ANNALS OF TENNESSEE.
   Sadie S. Patton, *"Hot Springs Famous Since 1778."* ASHEVILLE CITIZEN-TIMES, November 6, 1949.
   LEGENDS, Sally Royce Weir.

3. HISTORY OF 1783 — LAND GRANTS — WILLIAM NEILSON, SR.
   LAND GRANTS, BUNCOMBE AND MADISON COUNTY COURTHOUSE.
   JOHN GRAY BLOUNT, STOKLEY-DONALDSON GRANTS, U.S. FOREST SERVICE.
   William Neilson, Sr., Betsy Neilson, Neilson Historian.
   Old Love's Road, John Preston Arthur, *HISTORY OF WESTERN NORTH CAROLINA* (A HISTORY FROM 1730-1913). Published by The Edward Buncombe Chapter of DAR of Asheville, North Carolina, 1914 by E. H. D. Morrison 1914, p. 491.
   "Ferries," William Cullen Bryant, PICTURESQUE AMERICA, (edit. 1872) p. 46.

4. HISTORY 1786-1883 — WARM SPRINGS HOTEL — PATTON HOTEL
   "A Road to be Built up the French Broad Valley" SOME UNWRITTEN HISTORY. "How Greene County Embraced a Large Portion of North Carolina and How the Same Was Lost." by A. B. W., old 1899 Newspaper.
   "Spaightville," William Powell, THE NORTH CAROLINA GAZETTEER, University of North Carolina, Chapel Hill Press, 1968, p. 468.
   "Buncombe Turnpike, Built 1828," John Parris, ASHEVILLE CITIZEN, Asheville, N. C. September 3, 1989. Dick Kaplan, ASHEVILLE CITIZEN-TIMES, July 17, 1960.
   "Development of the First Hotel," Sadie Smathers Patton, FOUNDING STONES OF MADISON COUNTY, (Manuscript in North Carolina Department of Archives and History) Raleigh, North Carolina, January 1, 1951, p. 71.
   "Bishop Asbury's Visit," John Preston Arthur, HISTORY OF WESTERN NORTH CAROLINA (1730-1913) p. 219.

133

"Patton Hotel Damaged by Fire," Sadie S. Patton,"Hot Springs Famous Since 1778," ASHEVILLE CITIZEN-TIMES, November 6, 1949.

"Description of Patton Hotel," Charles Lanman, "Hot Springs — 100 Years Ago," THE STATE XXII, March 26, 1955, p. 14.

"Billy Vance, Manager of Hotel," Mary Ellen Wolcott, "Zeb Vance Once Clerked in Hotel at Hot Springs," ASHEVILLE TIMES, January 21, 1965. p. 5.

"Amusement of Hotel Guests Was to Explore a Cave," Sally Royce Weir, HOT SPRINGS, PAST AND PRESENT, S. B. Newman Press, Knoxville, Tennessee, 1906.

"Wade Hampton Cottage," Elizabeth Rumbough Dotterer. (Interview).

"Buncombe County Formed," NORTH CAROLINA GAZETTEER, p. 74.

5. RUMBOUGH — CIVIL WAR
"Rumbough and Powell Family," Elizabeth R. Dotterer, granddaughter of Colonel Rumbough, (Interview).

"James Henry Rumbough's House and Pictures," Richard Harrison Doughty, GREENEVILLE ONE HUNDRED YEAR PORTRAIT, 1775-1875. Published by Richard Harrison Doughty, p. 286.

"Civil War," Elizabeth R. Dotterer, (Interview).

"Civil War Medicine," Katherine M. Jones, HEROINES OF DIXIE, Published by the Bobbs, Merrill Company, Inc., p. 261.

"Major Beverly Hill," Henry Thomas Rumbough, SCRAPBOOK.

6. RUMBOUGH'S STAGE LINE RAILROAD — PATTON HOTEL BURNS
"Describing Stage Stops," John Preston Arthur, HISTORY OF WESTERN NORTH CAROLINA, p. 242.

"Rumbough Cuts Down Toll Gate," Elizabeth R. Dotterer. (Interview).

The Financing of the Railroad, Hugh T. Lefler, HISTORY OF NORTH CAROLINA. Lewis Historical Publishing Company, Inc., New York 1956, p. 627.

First Railroad to go Through the Southern Range of the Appalachian Mountains. John Preston Arthur, HISTORY OF WESTERN NORTH CAROLINA. pp. 71-72.

Patton Hotel Destroyed by Fire, Elizabeth R. Dotterer. (Interview).

Southern Improvement Company. (Ibid).

Laurel River and Hot Springs Railroad Company. HENRY THOMAS RUMBOUGH'S SCRAPBOOK.

7. MOUNTAIN PARK HOTEL — FAILURE OF MOUNTAIN PARK
Description of Mountain Park, Old Advertisement.

Social life of Hotel, Elizabeth R. Dotterer. (Interview).

Peter's Rock, John Preston Arthur, HISTORY OF WESTERN NORTH CAROLINA. (1730-1913). Published by Edward and Broughton, Chapter of Buncombe DAR of Asheville, North Carolina.

Dr. W. F. Ross, M.D., HOTEL RESORTS FOR THE SOUTH. Pack Memorial Library.

(Ref. N.C. Number 917, p. 334.)
Description of Mountain Park Hotel, Elizabeth R. Dotterer. (Interview).
Failure of Mountain Park Hotel. (Ibid.)
E. W. Grove, Bob Seymour, ASHEVILLE CITIZEN, November 21, 1961.
Colonel Rumbough sells hotel, Madison County Deed Book 30, p. 402.

8. FLOODS OF 1896, 1916, and 1977
Flood of 1896, HENRY THOMAS RUMBOUGH'S SCRAPBOOK.
Flood of 1916, Elizabeth R. Dotterer, Burder Fowler, and Iowa Melton. (Interviews).

9. KATE MAE (BESSIE) RUMBOUGH'S FIRST MARRIAGE
BESSIE RUMBOUGH JOHNSON'S MARRIAGE TO SAFFORD
The Johnson's wedding picture and Andrew Johnson, Jr., as a young boy.
Richard Harrison Doughty, *GREENEVILLE ONE HUNDRED YEAR PORTRAIT*,
    p. 257.
The first marriage, Elizabeth R. Dotterer, niece of Bessie. (Interview).
Andrew Johnson, Jr.'s visit to Hot Springs, when he escaped over the balcony.
    Elizabeth R. Dotterer. (Interview).
Bessie's Marriage to Daniel Bigelow Safford. Elizabeth R. Dotterer (Interview).
St. John's Catholic Church, Reverend Andrew V. Graves, S. J.

10. THE GARRETTS
Betsy Neilson, Neilson Historian.

11. GERMAN INTERNMENT — MOUNTAIN PARK HOTEL BURNS
Information on German ships. MADISON COUNTY PAPER, June 1, 1917, July 20,
    1917, and November 16, 1917.
German civilians, Elizabeth R. Dotterer. (Interview).
German Village, Photographs by Reverend Walker E. McBath, contributed by Mr.
    and Mrs. H. W. Close, Decatur, Georgia.
Welland Arnold Thompson delivering milk, contributed by his daughter, Naomi
    Thompson of Mechanicsburg, Pa.
Mountain Park Hotel Burns, HENRY THOMAS RUMBOUGH'S SCRAPBOOK.

12. BESSIE RUMBOUGH SAFFORD — NATIKA SAFFORD'S MARRIAGE — FAMOUS
    ENGINEER
Mrs. Safford's Building of Sanitorium, Elizabeth R. Dotterer. (Interview).
Jesuit Order of Missouri Province, Reverend Andrew V. Graves, S. J.
Natika's Marriage, Elizabeth R. Dotterer. (Interview).
Karen Stieke, Wembley, Alberta, Canada
Doreen Sieker Wembley, Alberta, Canada.
Annie (Johnson) Currie's ALONG THE WAPITA, p. 42.
Famous Engineer, HENRY THOMAS RUMBOUGH'S SCRAPBOOK.

INDEX